00224911

Gift Aid Donation

£1.

D1585383

LETTERS
FROM
SCHOOL

John Rae

COLLINS
8 Grafton Street, London W1
1987

William Collins Sons & Co. Ltd
London · Glasgow · Sydney · Auckland
Toronto · Johannesburg

BRITISH LIBRARY CATALOGUING IN PUBLICATION DATA

Rae, John, *1931*–
    Letters from school.
    1. School superintendents and principals—
    Great Britain
I. Title
    371.2´012´0941   LB2831.976.G7

ISBN 0 00 637105 1

Copyright © John Rae 1987

Photoset in Monophoto Plantin Light by
Ace Filmsetting Ltd, Frome, Somerset
Made and printed in Great Britain by
Robert Hartnoll (1985) Ltd, Bodmin

To
my grandson
JAMIE

'Education should be gentle and stern, not cold and lax'
– JOUBERT

CONTENTS

PREFACE

I wrote this book because I wanted parents to understand a headmaster's point of view.

The relationship between parents and their children's headmaster or headmistress is a strange one; so much remains unsaid. Behind the courtesies, the dinner parties and the brace of pheasants at Christmas, there are things that parents want to say to me but never do. I, too, pull my punches when it might be more helpful to say exactly what I think.

The parents' reluctance to speak their mind is understandable. My wife and I have six children and as they have made their rather haphazard way through the education system – both state and independent – we have felt a sense of impotence and frustration, as if they have been hostages in the hands of the school. As a teacher, I may recoil from the idea that parents dare not criticize too much for fear that their child will suffer. But as a parent I know that is true.

Just as parents are insecure in their relations with the school, teachers also feel insecure because theirs is the one job in society that everyone feels qualified to criticize. We have all been to school. We know how it's done. It didn't strike us then and it doesn't strike us now as a job requiring much in the way of sophisticated expertise. It isn't like medicine or law. We wouldn't actually say that any fool could do it but we think it is largely a question of common sense, an amateur business and not even full-time, given the long holidays and short working day.

It is precisely this view of teaching that makes teachers insecure and hypersensitive to criticism. Headmasters and headmistresses, too, are insecure, more so than they look.

They regard any criticism of the school as a criticism of their leadership, as indeed it is. There have been times when I have been unable to bring myself to read a parental letter of complaint. I have put it in a drawer and left it there for several hours, even days, until I felt calm enough to respond.

When parents are reluctant to voice their complaints and headmasters are reluctant to listen, it is not surprising that mutual understanding is imperfect. I do not mean to suggest that this is always the case; there are parents who have told me exactly what they thought and vice versa and I am sure that is true in all schools. But too often we are guarded in our exchanges and that is a pity, to say the least, because we are working for the same goal.

That is the thought that lies behind this book. I have written a series of letters on those topics that I know parents have wanted me to discuss openly with them. They are letters that I now feel free to write. But do not expect any startling revelations; I am not in the scandal business. The parents to whom the letters are written and the characters in the letters are imaginary. Like a novelist, I have created composite characters from aspects of the many pupils, teachers and parents I have known. As they used to say at the beginning of the Hollywood film, any similarity to persons, living or dead, is unintentional.

The incidents described in the letters are drawn from many schools, not just from those with which I have been associated. Some are based on real incidents, with details changed; others are imaginary. All are true to life in the sense that they are the sorts of incidents that all headmasters know can and do occur.

The one invariably true aspect of the letters is my own reaction to people and events. This is how a headmaster thought and felt and acted. I have made no attempt to disguise my prejudices or to present my reactions to the various problems as a consistent philosophy of education. If I have such a philosophy it is that education is too dependent on the inconsistency, the quirkiness of personality to be reduced to a theoretical model. This book is about the practice of education not the theory.

How can a theory do justice to the variety of responses to a particular teacher – scorned by some of his pupils, admired by others – or to the disconcerting truth that where a conscientious teacher makes little impression, a self-centred, inflexible man whose idiosyncrasies border on the insane, can inspire his pupils with a deep and lasting love of his subject? Education theory does not, indeed cannot, account for such peculiarities.

I enjoy speculating on the mysteries of education but that is not the same as laying down theories. Why, for example, does a sixteen-year-old boy discover – overnight it seems – the motivation to develop his talents when for so long he has been in the doldrums? Who or what triggered the unexpected surge? And why in his case does it occur at sixteen, when in others it occurs at fourteen or twenty-four or never occurs at all? We can speculate but we cannot find a law or theory that will enable us to predict when or whether this all-important discovery of motivation will occur. Education is not and never will be an exact science.

Because I wanted to write about the practice of education I have relied as far as possible on my own experience. That has been almost exclusively in independent schools in the United Kingdom, though I taught for a brief spell in New York and have visited schools and talked with pupils and teachers in many parts of the world. I have never taught in a fully co-educational school, though I have for many years taught girls in the sixth form at Westminster. My illustrations are taken from one type of school and I refer for the most part to headmasters and boys, but the topics discussed in these letters will be familiar to all parents and to anyone who knows about schools. The problems of education are universal.

*

Dear Parents

If you don't believe everything your child tells you about school, I will not believe everything your child tells me about home.

Yours sincerely

JOHN RAE

VALUE FOR MONEY

Dear Mr Ormond

Thank you for your suggestion that we should call in a firm of management consultants to show us where we can 'cut our costs and give parents better value for money'.

It's true that the fees are high here, though no higher than those for comparable schools. Whether they could be lower depends not only on the efficiency of the operation but also on educational policy. For example, it is usually not cost effective to offer a minority subject such as Russian because one master may be employed to teach only a handful of pupils. On the other hand, the educational policy of the school may be to offer precisely those subjects that are not available at most schools.

Whether we give value for money is a question which can be asked of all schools whether independent or maintained. In relation to the maintained sector the question is asked at the national level; is society getting value for money in the schools it is paying for? In the independent sector it is asked of a particular school. Either way it is a difficult question to answer which is why educationalists avoid it.

Let me first deal with the easier question: whether schools are as efficiently managed as they should be. I am talking about independent, fee-paying schools but many of the same arguments apply to those maintained by the local education authority. There is no free education in this country or in any other country for that matter. Education costs money. It is just a question of whether the costs are met directly out of fees or indirectly by rates and taxes. I think the independent school, responsible for its own finances and having to compete for customers in the market, is more likely to be efficiently managed and to give value for money. Whether I am right, I leave you to judge.

An independent school like this can only charge the level of fees that it believes the market will bear. That means that our fees must be roughly in line with our competitors'. When you were shopping around for schools for Richard, I am sure it did not escape your notice that the more famous schools charged fees similar to and sometimes even below those of the smaller, less-well-known schools. In some cases that is because the famous schools are well endowed and use their endowment income to subsidize fees. But the more important reason is that the costs of education do not vary from school to school. What the endowment income enables the richer school to do is to offer a more varied menu at the same price. In this sense a well-endowed school, such as Eton, is bound to offer parents better value for money, unless it is badly managed. But most independent schools have to live off their fees and fees reflect pretty accurately what it costs to run the school. The largest single item in the budget is the salaries of the teaching staff. In a boarding school that accounts for 35 per cent of expenditure; in a day school, where the other costs are much lower, the figure is nearer 50 per cent. Education is such a labour-intensive business, the only effective way to cut costs is to reduce the salary bill.

In theory, we could freeze or even reduce our teachers' salaries. They are paid on a different scale from teachers in the maintained sector and on the whole they are paid better. But they are not well paid. A young man or woman joining us straight from university this year, 1986, will earn around £8000 a year gross. That is not bad, though his university

18

contemporaries going into the City may earn twice as much. But it is in their salary prospects that teachers are at such a disadvantage. The young man in the City will be earning £20,000 within a very few years whereas the teacher at the most affluent independent schools will not reach £20,000 even after twenty-five or thirty years' service. In other words a teacher is not earning at sixty what many of the boys he taught are earning before they are thirty.

We could pay our teachers less but to what end? We should lose their goodwill and lose our edge in the market for good staff. Value for money is partly a question of our being in a position to attract the best teachers. The successful, well-endowed independent schools are the Liverpools and Manchester Uniteds of the academic world: they can afford to buy the players they need. There is, for example, a national shortage of qualified, competent teachers of mathematics. I will go to almost any lengths to get a good mathematician: head-hunt, outbid the rival buyers, offer inducements such as subsidized housing and free education for his children. (We haven't gone in for 'golden hallos' yet but I would not be surprised to hear soon that a promising mathematician had been offered a signing-on fee.) As the headmaster of an independent school I have more freedom than the head of a comprehensive to pitch my salary offer at an attractive level but I have to work within the scale laid down by the governors. That scale is not over-generous, so please don't ask me to cut costs that way.

A more realistic approach would be to cut the number of teachers – indeed, that is arguably the only way in which significant economies can be made in education. When the Government has to make education cuts, teachers' jobs have to go. When I visited a comprehensive school in Corby last year, the headmaster told me that he had been told by the local education authority to 'lose' two members of staff at the end of the school year. He had decided to lose the two teachers

million in new buildings and facilities. As you are well aware, a large part of that figure will have been contributed by current parents.

As far as the other costs are concerned, Richard would no doubt confirm that you are not paying for cordon bleu catering; in a boarding school, catering accounts for no more than 10 per cent of expenditure. The rest of the money goes on teaching materials, games, running costs, maintenance and administration. So that in a school such as this, which is partly boarding and partly day, expenditure can be broken down as follows.

	%
Teachers' salaries including superannuation	42.0
Other salaries and wages	19.3
	61.3
Catering	9.7
Rent, rates, fuel and light	8.2
Maintenance	8.1
Teaching materials and games	5.3
Miscellaneous including interest on debts	4.5
Administration	2.9
	38.7
	100.0

Have we got the distribution right? One way we check is to compare our breakdown with that of comparable schools. A number of major chartered accountants' firms offer a service in cost controls and provide comparative figures of other schools. We use these services. It is understandable that parents who work in the commercial world should believe that academic institutions must be – almost by definition – run in an amateur or just incompetent manner. But was it ever true of the independent schools? If so, how have they managed not only to survive but flourish for so long? This can't just be put down to the failings of the maintained sector. There must be some shrewd management in there somewhere.

I accept that in education it is possible to get away with incompetence for longer than in the commercial world because success and failure are less easy to measure; or to put it another way, failure takes longer to bite. But if an independent school's costs are not kept under tight control, the amateurism will soon show itself in fee increases that are out of line. If you see a school shooting up to the top of the fee league (where paradoxically it will acquire fame rather than notoriety, for in the snob world expensiveness carries with it a certain cachet) you can be fairly sure that the previous twelve months witnessed some financial mismanagement.

When an independent school overspends on its budget and has to claw back the money by a sharp increase in fees, this can often be attributed not only to bad management but also to a clash of personality. The management structure of an independent school is odd, to put it mildly. The chief executive is the headmaster but he does not have financial control or even financial responsibility. The financial management is in the hands of the bursar who, in most schools, is directly responsible to the governing body, not to the headmaster. It is a situation ripe for conflict and misunderstanding. At its worst, the headmaster regards the bursar as ignorant of education and resents his power to influence education policies, while the bursar regards the headmaster as ignorant of finance and resents his power to advocate policies without regard to their financial implications. Both appeal to the governors, the ultimate authority, who rather enjoy seeing the headmaster and bursar at loggerheads but often lack the knowledge of the school or the political skills required to reconcile the two protagonists. That is the situation at its worst. In most schools, headmasters and bursars learn to work together but a clash of personality or failure of communication between headmaster and bursar can throw the school's finances into disarray.

My impression is that nowadays financial mismanagement

in independent schools is rare. I doubt whether the most searching investigation by your management consultants would conclude that 'this educational package could be produced more cheaply'.

Even so, I am surprised parents do not ask more questions especially about the other costs which appear unexpectedly on the bill. I think some of the practices operated by independent schools would be called sharp in a commercial context. There can be a considerable difference between the published fees and the amount parents have to pay. Statements in the prospectus that 'other expenses are kept to a minimum' are not infrequently misleading. At some schools 'extras' amount to £300 to £500 a year at 1986 prices. Schools get away with it because parents, unlike the diners in a restaurant or the passengers on an airline, cannot with total conviction threaten to take their custom elsewhere. Once their child enters the school, they are committed, or trapped, depending on which way you look at it. If I were a prospective parent I would ask to see not only the annual fees but a typical term's bill for a boy in his first year and a boy in his final year so that I could check what the school regards as 'extras'. If, to take just one example, games fixtures are part of the educational package, the school should pay the travel expenses instead of charging them to the parents of boys selected to play.

As you say, it is 'a hell of an expensive business', but it is not as expensive as it would be if the school did not enjoy charitable status. If, as the Labour Party threatens, that status was removed, the fees would rise by 8 to 10 per cent. As a charity we pay only 50 per cent of the rates as well as enjoying other tax concessions. For some parents, the fees are reduced in other ways. 18 per cent of pupils at independent schools are receiving financial help, in most cases from the school itself in the form of scholarships awarded on academic merit or bursaries given where financial hardship hits the parents during the boy's school career. There are surprisingly few of the latter cases, perhaps because our parents tend to be the ones who make other people redundant. On the other hand I suspect that some astute parents take the schools for a ride. I know of one instance where the parents of a girl left their smart car and elegant clothes at home and travelled to the school by train in modest style and clothes suggesting the thrifty lower-middle class, to which they certainly did not belong. The headmistress was impressed by their determination to do their best for their daughter. 'Even if you cannot help, Headmistress, we will make every sacrifice to send Julia to you because we are convinced it is the right school for her.' The headmistress gave the girl a substantial bursary. It was some months later that the headmistress was told that the plain signature on the registration form hid the heir to an Irish peerage. Financial checks? Statements of income? Yes, we do require such information, but how can you be sure that parents are telling the whole truth? In the USA, independent schools require parents asking for financial help to produce their latest tax returns. That is more businesslike.

For the majority of parents who are paying the full fees, plus all the extras, a ten-year commitment to the independent sector is quite an investment. How do they manage to raise that sort of money?

Our schools are not the preserves of the super-rich (I reckon that 1 per cent, that is six out of six hundred fathers of pupils here are multi-millionaires) but they are almost exclusively for the children of parents whose incomes are at least double the national average. The idea that anyone can afford an independent education if they give up foreign holidays is a myth. It is also a myth that in many cases fees are paid out of grandparents' capital. As far as we can tell, most parents are paying school fees out of income. They may, through the various schemes available, spread the cost over a long period. They may have two incomes, with mother working during the years the children are at school. But they are paying out of income nevertheless.

Is it true – as you imply – that these parents are making a

sacrifice? Not in the sense of the widow who works all night to ensure that her children will eat. It is not that sort of sacrifice, though some parents like to present it as such, particularly to their children. I have no doubt that most parents who pay school fees are denying themselves something but so they do to pay the mortgage. School fees are an investment that pays off not in cash but in our pride and happiness in our children's achievement. I had a letter recently which read: '— is doing well at St Mary's. After a slightly shaky start he has settled down to some hard work and goes for an honours viva in Pathology next month. His education at your school is paying off.' Is it value for money? It depends on what you think you are paying for. If your main concern is to rescue your child from the risks of state education then you should be happy to pay the cost of alternative schooling. But of course for most parents rescue is not enough. They have to be convinced that private schooling has positive advantages.

If I pay for private health care I know exactly what I am buying: treatment by the physician or surgeon of my choice, at a time to suit me and in a private room at the hospital or clinic. I am not paying for a better chance of recovery or cure; I am paying to make the business of ill-health less disagreeable than it would otherwise be.

With private education there is a fundamental difference. I am not paying just to make my children's experience of schooling less disagreeable. I am hoping to buy the education equivalent of a better chance of recovery or cure; in other words, I am hoping that private education will give my children a better start in life. I can't guarantee this result because education is such an unpredictable process. I could pay £6000 a year and end up with my son or daughter patently worse educated than if they had gone to the local comprehensive. So there is an element of risk in my investment and yours. Don't ask me the odds. There are too many variables. But the evidence for the success of private education is overwhelming. Almost every parent in this country who can afford to do so chooses to send his child to a private school. They can't all be snobs. On the contrary, most are shrewd men of business and affairs who have calculated the probable advantages and invested accordingly. And it is precisely because the Labour Party believes those advantages exist that it is so intent on attacking private schools. The socialist rhetoric – 'privilege', 'unfairness', 'injustice' – is the compliment that they pay us.

I suppose that in the end the best you can say about value for money is that if it works it's worth it. You may remember Somerset Maugham's comment on sex: 'No woman is worth more than £5 unless you are in love with her and then she is worth all you've got.' If a school doesn't work for your child, it isn't worth a fiver, though you will have paid a lot more than that, if only through rates and taxes. But if it does work, if Richard's potential really has been developed, if he eventually looks back on his schooldays with pleasure but not nostalgia, if he is a confident, independent spirit not a frightened conformist, if, in other words, he has all the makings of a young man not an overgrown schoolboy – then it will have been worth if not all you've got, at least the fees you will have had to pay. Good education is priceless.

Yours sincerely

JOHN RAE

2

CLASSROOM DISCIPLINE

Dear Peter

Your letter caught me on the raw. You say that 'the standard of discipline in the school has declined significantly in the last few years', but what is your evidence? It amounts to this. Jonathan has told you that 'lots of masters have difficulty keeping order in the classroom'.

Before dealing with that allegation let me tell you why, as a headmaster, I find sweeping generalizations about bad discipline irritating yet difficult to take seriously.

We all know how to discipline other people's children. It is only when we have to discipline our own that the right approach is less easy to identify and carry out. When it comes to schools, better discipline is almost invariably what parents, old boys and governors say they would like to see. When I left Harrow to become headmaster of Taunton, the Governors of Taunton took me on one side to tell me that I would have to tighten up the discipline. When I left Taunton to become headmaster of Westminster, the Governors of Westminster gave me the same advice. When I left Westminster, the same governors told my successor that one of his priorities must be to improve the discipline.

I would not have been surprised to hear that all incoming headmasters and headmistresses are told that discipline needs tightening. It has probably been the same for generations. The reasons are obvious enough. Adult anxiety about the discipline of the young is a recurring theme partly because we know that a framework of discipline is essential to the business of growing up, and partly because we fear the anarchy that youthful indiscipline implies. There is a sense in which all our hopes and fears for the young concentrate in that one word, 'discipline'. When we are uncertain what it is exactly that worries us about the state of a school or the state of society, we attack the lack of discipline. It is such an easy target. Do you know Edmund Burke's comment on pacifist literature: 'A commonplace against war; the easiest of all topics'? The armchair disciplinarian also shoots at easy targets. That is why I find it difficult to take him seriously. Nevertheless your letter caught me on the raw – as no doubt it was intended to do! Discipline is the touchstone of a headmaster's authority; if his authority is undermined he has to go. His career is over. That is why, unless he has lost confidence altogether, he will fight against any suggestion that discipline is slack.

It is quite untrue that 'lots of masters have difficulty keeping order'. I know of two cases, that is two out of fifty. I am not suggesting that a small number of weak masters can be ignored; if Jonathan is not learning any mathematics because Mr Anderson cannot keep control it makes no difference whether Mr Anderson is unique or typical. For the individual pupil what matters is whether that teacher in that subject is capable of maintaining good order. If you had complained specifically about Mr Anderson you would have been right to do so. You may not think so but headmasters welcome specific complaints because it strengthens their hand in doing something about it. It is very tempting for a headmaster to put off dealing with a member of staff who is reported to be having problems in the classroom. You hope the problem will go away. The parent's complaint is both useful evidence and a timely reminder that some action has to be taken. Looking back over my years of headmastering, I wish parents had complained more on this specific issue of classroom discipline.

I am astonished that my parents never complained of the classroom chaos that characterized my early education in the war years. But then as a parent *I* didn't complain, even when I knew that some of our children's teachers were hopelessly inadequate at keeping order. I suppose I was embarrassed about putting a colleague on the spot. A lame excuse. I should have complained; by not doing so I was failing in my duty as a parent.

So you and I will agree on this point at least: good order in the classoom is essential to good learning. Where we do not agree is on your assertion that this school's discipline has deteriorated. I accept that since learning is the chief object of any school, the quality of classroom discipline is the best guide to the quality of discipline in the school as a whole. If there is chaos in the classrooms no amount of spit and polish will make a school well disciplined. But there is all the difference in the world between one or two masters experiencing difficulty and the whole school being ill disciplined.

I have been a headmaster for twenty years and I have never known a time when there was not one member of my staff having difficulty in the classroom. Every head would like to have a perfect team. But it doesn't happen. The difference between a good school and a bad one is that in the former the number of weak teachers is very small and the headmaster is doing all he can to limit the damage.

What exactly can he do about it?

The two teachers here who are having difficulties represent two of the common causes of discipline problems in the classroom. Mr Anderson you know. He is a young man in his first year of teaching; he is learning the trade. Mr Ritchie has never taught Jonathan but you may have met him at a parents' evening. He is within two years of retirement and after thirty years on the staff he has lost interest. A harsher critic might say that he has lost his nerve.

Imagine a lion-tamer in a circus. Whatever the tricks of the trade, once he is alone in the cage with the lions, his authority is all that keeps the animals at bay. If the lions sense that he has lost his nerve they will turn on him.

For the teacher alone in the classroom, survival is also a battle of wills. A young teacher who does not understand this will be eaten alive. Curiously enough, I find that parents recognize the truth of this more readily than some teachers who think it possible to establish an atmosphere of co-operation without the exercise of authority. A teacher who fails to establish his authority will never enjoy teaching or the respect of his pupils. It has always been thus and I cannot see that it will ever change. The medieval schoolmaster faced with very large classes, very long hours and a very tedious curriculum kept control by the liberal use of the rod. The modern teacher may feel that he is part of a more humane and enlightened education system, but while the nature of punishment and the curriculum may change, the nature of pupils does not. When I was at school, the standard way to break up a tedious lesson was to con the teacher into letting you leave the room. 'Please, sir, may I be excused?' An Oxford schoolmaster teaching in the year 1500 had to deal with the same tactics. 'As soon as I am cum into the scole,' he complained, 'this fellow goith to make water.'

Boys and girls don't change. It is no good appealing to their better nature. Young lions cannot be expected to see things from the tamer's point of view. Nor is it any good warning them that unless they behave they will fail their exams. That may worry some of them individually but collectively they are interested in the here and now. They expect a teacher to exert his authority and earn their respect. If he fails, no amount of sweet reasoning or dire warnings will save him.

My job is to help a young teacher like Mr Anderson understand this simple reality. Anderson took a good degree in mathematics at Oxford and did a postgraduate certificate of education at London. He has had teaching practice in a mixed comprehensive in Eltham but this is his first teaching post. He has a lot going for him: a pleasant, open personality, a sense of humour and an enthusiasm for his subject. I have no doubt that he will become a very good teacher. But it will take longer than it might have done because he fell into the trap of thinking that he could keep order by establishing a relaxed and friendly relationship with the boys. So he could, but only if he had first established his authority.

When he arrived last September I talked through the problem of discipline with him. I told him how important it was to learn the boys' names quickly; if you cannot be bothered to learn a boy's name, why should he be bothered to do what you say? I also told him to plan his lessons because a teacher who knows where he is going is less easy to blow off course. Above all, I told him to be strict first and friendly later. I read him this advice from a book written by an Eton Master, Arthur Benson, in 1902:

> The power of maintaining discipline is the *unum necessarium* for a teacher; if he has not got it and cannot acquire it, he had better sweep a crossing. It insults the soul, it is destructive of all self-respect and dignity to be incessantly at the mercy of boys. They are merciless and the pathos of the situation never touches them at all.

Mr Anderson did not take Benson's advice or mine. No doubt he thought times had changed. He was so close to the boys in age he thought he understood them better. He could not believe that they were merciless. Treat them as equals and they would treat you as a friend. The result of this optimistic policy Jonathan has told you.

Your difficulty as a parent is that your son is suffering from Anderson's lack of experience. You want something done about it straight away. My difficulty is that I believe in Anderson's potential but cannot turn him into a good disciplinarian overnight. You want action and I need time. We face a problem familiar to parents and head teachers all over the world. How can we reconcile the interests of the pupil and the needs of an inexperienced teacher?

Your letter suggests one solution. If Mr Anderson can't cope he should be sacked. You say, 'If a commercial or industrial concern tolerated incompetence to the same degree as schools, it would soon go out of business.' Schools are slow to weed out incompetent teachers, that is true. But in all walks of life the young man or woman is given a chance to learn from mistakes. The difference between teaching and your business, for example, is that the young teacher *has* to be thrown in at the deep end. He cannot spend six months moving from one department to another and shadowing senior men. Even if schools could afford to give a young teacher that period of grace I doubt whether it would help much. There is no substitute for being alone in the classroom. The sooner a teacher goes solo the better.

Then it is up to the head of department and the headmaster to see that he does not crash. That is the stage we are at with Mr Anderson. The head of department is telling him how to deal with the rowdiest boys, of which I gather Jonathan is one. Sorry! That was difficult to resist, but it has a serious purpose too. Anderson has been told that if a boy flatly refuses to do what he is told he must be sent to me. That may lead to Jonathan's being suspended for a short time as a warning to others as well as to himself. I hope it does not happen because I do not like using the headmaster's authority to solve a teacher's classroom problems unless there is no other way. On the other hand, Mr Anderson is too promising a teacher for me to let his career here fail because one mathematics set is out of control.

When I started teaching at Harrow the headmaster, Dr James, rescued me in a similar manner. One form of fifteen-year-olds almost had me on the run. The ringleader was an Irish boy called Michael. Nothing I could do seemed to have any effect on him. He was taking me on and the rest of the form aided and abetted him while watching to see who would win. I knew that if I lost, I would almost certainly have to leave Harrow, perhaps give up teaching altogether. Is there any other job in which your quality is tested so searchingly, so soon? The struggle continued for the best part of my first term. I would lie awake at night planning a decisive blow and when I slept the classroom was not infrequently the scene of anxious dreams. Do pupils know how much they haunt their teacher's midnight hours?

Then Dr James called me in. A parent had complained. James told me that if there was no other way I should send the ringleader to him. Somehow I knew that he really did not expect me to do so. It was a gesture of support. 'Good luck,' he said as I went out.

I entered the classroom for the next lesson more relaxed and more confident, knowing that I would go to almost any lengths to solve the problem without sending the boy to the headmaster. It was just the stimulus I needed. When Michael launched into the attack, my heart beat faster but it was excitement, not fear. I took him on but I made a point of not punishing him. He must have sensed my determination for although his attacks did not cease at once, they began to lose their force and their conviction. The form distanced themselves from him. 'Oh shut up, Michael', I heard more than once. The balance of power was shifting in my favour. It took several weeks but I knew that I would win and so did he. Towards the end, his interventions became increasingly half-hearted as though he wished to give the impression that he did not care whether or not they succeeded in interrupting the lesson. By the end of term the whole form had come into line. Did you know that when a farmer lets heifers into a field, they always start by running round the fences? If they find a weak point they push at it until they break through. If they don't, they settle down and never bother with the fence again.

So give me time to mend the fence. If I do not succeed by the end of term I shall have to take a different course. There are teachers who will never learn the art of keeping discipline. There are others who, having failed in one school, will have no problems in the next. You may remember that this happened to Mr Chips. He couldn't keep order in his first school. When he moved to Brookfield, his new headmaster told him: 'Never mind, you're full young; it's largely a matter of experience. You have another chance here. Take up a firm attitude from the beginning, that's the secret of it.'

There *are* some hopeless cases – hopeless and pathetic in the literal sense of being pitiable. When does a case become hopeless? There was a young Latin master whose lack of control was such that every time he turned to write on the blackboard, the boys threw india rubbers at the back of his head. When they tired of this sport, they tried to bounce the rubbers off the blackboard on to his face. A headmaster might just have been able to save the man when the rubbers were hitting the back of the head but had no hope once they started hitting the face! If a man has so little self-respect that he allows that to happen, he had better get out of teaching as fast as he can.

I sometimes wonder whether those who regard teaching as a soft option have any idea what it is like to be shut in a classroom with pupils who are after your blood. It is the subject of some good comic scenes in film and fiction but it is no joke if your job and perhaps your career depend on the outcome. How many of those who call for tougher discipline in schools would survive ten minutes with a difficult adolescent form in full cry?

To which you will reply: it is the teacher's job to keep order, not mine. Right, but it's a job that requires more skill and nerve than perhaps you appreciate. You and I have both commanded a platoon of infantrymen. That was an easy job compared with trying to control a class of sixteen-year-olds.

In the army, your authority is sustained by military discipline and by the non-commissioned officers who relieve you of the rough and tumble of imposing order on the men. School discipline should underpin the teacher's authority but he has no non-commissioned officers to prowl between the desks. The teacher's authority is his own: the army officer's authority depends on factors outside himself. The army officer does not hesitate to see himself as an expert on discipline yet he probably knows less about it than the average teacher. Strange, isn't it? – the schoolmaster in his threadbare jacket may have more real authority than the colonel riding on his high horse.

I think Mr Anderson has the qualities of character to develop his own authority. Mr Ritchie had authority and lost it. For thirty years he kept good order and taught good history. Now, at the age of fifty-eight, he has been struck by a form of impotence, unforeseen, inexplicable and humiliating. He is having serious discipline problems with an O-level history set, problems he has not experienced since his first years of teaching. He came to see me last week and asked me to take the set away from him. He was angry and embarrassed. He refused to believe he had lost the knack. Like you, he claimed that there had been a decline in standards of discipline in the school. He believed that his difficulties arose not from any inadequacy of his own but from the failure of his colleagues, particularly his younger colleagues, to impose the standards of behaviour that he demanded. He saw himself as the commander of an outpost increasingly endangered by the collapse of less professional units. It was a comforting but inaccurate reading of the situation.

I have taken the O-level set away from him because I suspect that with those boys he has lost his nerve. Or perhaps it is simply that they have called his bluff. For some years his position as respected senior master has protected him, but now a new generation of boys who are ignorant or scornful of his special status is treating him like any other teacher and he does not know how to respond. It is sad to see this happen but it is a reminder that a teacher can never take his pupils' respect for granted. When I had been headmastering for fifteen years, I took a form of fifteen-year-olds for English while a colleague was on sabbatical leave. I thought it would be a pleasant change from A-level history and a welcome escape from administration. I made the mistake of not planning my lessons, imagining that the old pro could teach brilliantly off the cuff. Once the aura of the headmaster had worn off, the boys became restless. The lessons did not have a sense of direction. I had to raise my voice to keep the form quiet. With dismay I realized that I was allowing my authority to slip and that I would have to make a positive effort to regain respect and control. I could not punish them because it was unthinkable that the headmaster should have to put a boy in detention for misbehaving in class. What did I do? Mundane things you will think. I started insisting that the boys stand up when I entered the room (not the tradition in this school); any boy who was a moment late reported to me at some unearthly hour in the morning; anyone who spoke out of turn was chewed off in no uncertain terms; and formality characterized every aspect from the straight backs to the silent departure row by row when the bell rang. I felt I was parodying a French village schoolmaster of the turn of the century, stiff and humourless, and ready to pounce on the slightest flicker of rebellion. Was it wishful thinking that the pupils rather enjoyed it all? Not entirely. They prefer an orderly classroom because it protects them from the extroverts and loud-mouths who dominate a free-for-all; and they would rather a teacher played the pedagogue than pretended to be one of the boys. As for me, I had learnt the oldest lesson: 'Take up a firm attitude from the beginning. That's the secret of it.'

I don't believe that Mr Ritchie can recover his authority. The news that he is only a paper tiger has reached the other sets he teaches. I do not particularly like the man and I know that he does not like me. But I will do everything in my power to prevent his career ending in a mixture of farce and failure. If I succeed he may yet retire from the fray with some dignity. If I fail, the bitterness will sour a lonely, bachelor retirement. And remember, the pathos of the situation will not touch the boys at all. Nor should it. The lions are not responsible for their tamer's peace of mind.

So, Peter, there you are. It is not always as easy as you might think for the headmaster to guarantee perfect discipline in every classroom. Two members of staff who are having problems keeping order does not mean that 'the standard of discipline has declined significantly'. As you will have gathered, I think Mr Anderson has survival qualities. Let us give him a chance. Not a chance to ruin Jonathan's hopes of a good grade in O-level maths next year, but a chance to prove he can establish his authority. I will monitor the situation and so will you. If he succeeds, you will buy me a drink. If he fails, there will be nothing to celebrate.

Yours sincerely

JOHN RAE

PS I meant to tell you what happened to the young Latin master whose form bounced rubbers off the blackboard on to his face. I had to tell him to go. When the form heard this they clubbed together and bought him a leaving present. It was an antiquarian edition of Ovid's Poems. He showed it to me with an air of triumph, as though it was evidence that the boys had liked him all along. I did not disillusion him. He took a job in the civil service and I hear that he is doing well.

3

SCRUFFY, ILL-MANNERED AND FOUL-MOUTHED

Dear Brigadier Annesley

You and I have agreed on many things in the past, not only those that affected Mark's schooling but wider educational issues too. I have enjoyed our discussions and now that Mark is leaving I shall miss them. It is not true that headmastering is a lonely job but it is a job that, more than most, dictates your relationship with other people. So much of a headmaster's social life is spent in the company of interested parties, particularly parents, that there are very few disinterested conversations. That is why I have valued your friendship so much.

On one issue, however, we have never agreed. When it came up at the Petersons' last night you seized your last chance to corner me. I don't blame you for that. I didn't have the energy for that sort of argument over the dinner table in the last week of term, but I cannot let our paths divide without trying to convince you that I am not the permissive headmaster you take me to be.

What was it Peterson said? 'A school is only as good as its reputation.' You came in so promptly it might have been a cue. 'Your school has two reputations, Headmaster,' you said, and, knowing what was coming I could have kicked you under the table, 'a reputation for academic excellence that is unsurpassed and a less flattering reputation for allowing its pupils to be scruffy, ill-mannered and foul-mouthed.' I rather think you said 'encouraging' not 'allowing', but I will give you the benefit of the doubt!

Scruffy is a good word; the sound exactly conveys the image. In matters of school dress, a headmaster has to decide what he will not tolerate and then hold to that line as consistently as he can. If he swings about with every critical blast from parents or colleagues, his edicts will have little conviction. In practice my tactics are reminiscent of trench warfare: short bursts of activity – the boys call them blitzes – followed by long periods of watchful inertia. During a blitz, every shirt-tail is tucked in, every top button done up, every tie straightened, every ill-kempt head of hair given a sense of direction. It doesn't last long and the ground gained will be lost, but like a jerk on the lead it keeps the animal on course!

Parents face the same problem, not wanting to nag the whole time yet unwilling to abandon the struggle altogether. They care what their offspring look like but they have to decide how many tantrums, slammed doors and fruitless arguments a tidy appearance is worth. It's a losing battle but as a parent I console myself with the words of the senior master at Trinity School in New York. That school has no uniform, only a dress code which gives rise to numerous demarcation disputes because the code is open to so many interpretations. When is a jean not a jean? The senior master appealed to his colleagues for help. 'We cannot expect to win,' he told them, 'but let us at least go down to an honourable defeat.'

I care what the pupils look like, though in your opinion not enough. You would like to see every boy neat and tidy. I know there will always be some disaffected sixteen-year-olds who will defeat the system, and I am not willing to concentrate all the resources of the school's authority to bring them into line. So I settle for a majority of tidy boys and a minority of scarecrows. It is conscious policy, not, as you put it in one of your less generous moments, 'a loss of nerve'.

It has its disadvantages. The scruffiest boys always seem to gather in prominent positions, like shags on a rock, when parents or old boys visit the school. On one occasion I employed a trusted colleague to go ahead of me when I was showing round a distinguished prospective parent. His job was to sweep out of the way any scruffy or disaffected boys so that our tour of the school would reveal only bright and eager individuals purposefully engaged on out-of-school activities. It worked well, though my visitor remarked on the small number of boys we came across. I took him to one of the housemasters' for tea, the signal for my colleague to go off duty. It was a foolish mistake. As we said goodbye to the housemaster and set off across the courtyard towards the official car, there appeared in front of us a boy who was without exception the scruffiest in the school. Every item of his clothing, from his dirty old raincoat to his winklepicker shoes, seemed to have been chosen to give the maximum offence. He slunk past without so much as a flicker of recognition and disappeared into the bowels of a boarding house. I glanced at my distinguished visitor's face. The damage had been done. The son was sent to Harrow.

If you knew the feelings of impotent rage headmasters experience on such an occasion you would not say they do not care enough. But I find it difficult to take the subject as seriously as you do. I think you see too close a connection between what the pupils look like and the morale and efficiency of the school. But in some schools as in some armies – think of the Israelis – the efficiency of the operation seems to have little connection with the smartness of the 'troops'. You yourself told me that Napoleon's infantry gave the appearance of being dishevelled and undisciplined but in reality were the finest fighting force the world had seen. I could take you to schools where every pupil is spick and span, not in England but in South Africa and Australia. I have seen them and I liked what I saw. There is something reassuring about well-turned out schoolchildren; they are less threatening. But I found nothing in those schools to suggest that the superficial impression of excellence was reflected in the schools' achievement. The boys here may look dishevelled and undisciplined but they could not achieve the best academic results in the country unless morale and efficiency were high.

You say the boys are ill-mannered. What is your evidence? The same accusation was made at a governing body meeting recently but when I asked what exactly the governors had in mind, no one was able to say. 'There is a general agreement', one governor told me, 'that the manners of the boys leave a lot to be desired.' They probably do. A community of six hundred adolescents is not likely to be a model of civility.

There is, however, an underlying ideal of good manners that I think it is worth trying to get across. In *The Canterbury Tales*, Chaucer says of the Knight, 'He ne no villainye y said, in all his life, unto no manner wight', which I take to mean he was never rude to anyone, in other words he treated every person with equal courtesy regardless of rank. That is what I mean by good manners. Many people who complain about the bad manners of the young do not hesitate to treat with contempt those they regard as inferior. For such people good manners are not an ideal but a convenience. They want people to be polite to them and they are polite to the people they respect or need. They expect something in return, even if it is only a reputation for good manners. The young are right to see such manners as hypocritical but wrong to think the world can do without them. People can be disagreeable enough without encouraging them to be blunt.

In manners, there is the ideal and the convenient but the latter is shallow and insincere without the former, so parents and teachers have to communicate the importance of both. If it is hard-going sometimes, it is only because in the storms of adolescence you do not have much time or inclination to consider the feelings of others. Your own feelings are all-absorbing. At the same time you are in revolt against adult convention of which manners are the most obvious manifestation.

None of this prevents the young from being well-mannered when it suits them and in that sense they are already almost adult. For the most part they lead double lives: charming at one moment, bloody rude the next; polite as individuals, boorish in a group; cheerful at school, grumpy at home (or vice versa). 'I just do not recognize the boy you are describing,' was a father's response to the news that his son, who was so polite and patient with his invalid grandparents, had been punished for spitting at an unpopular master.

The pattern of manners is set at a young age and I doubt whether it can be altered much during the teenage years, however turbulent these may be. The rules of the game are laid down in childhood, flouted in adolescence and re-established in adulthood. Many of the rules of manners I obey date from my parents' teaching nearly half a century ago. Though my father is dead the thought that he would have disapproved can still act as a check.

If manners are so firmly established in childhood we should not get too excited by the ill-mannered adolescent or exaggerate the influence schools can have. I do not mean that schools can opt out of their responsibility for good manners but their role is more a question of keeping the show on the road than writing the original script.

Yet how difficult it can be to keep a sense of perspective! I hope Mark has infuriated you at times so that you know how it feels. A headmaster cannot afford to lose his cool. He can be angry but not ill-tempered. But there have been occasions on which I would gladly have struck a boy whose gross bad manners provoked me. If parents of teenage children experience the same temptation they should be reassured that it is normal. But it is a temptation we must resist. On the other hand I do not think an outburst of anger does any harm even when – or especially when – that is precisely what the bad manners were designed to provoke. There is something unnatural about parents who are so laid back they cannot be provoked.

Some complaints about boys' bad manners provoke me more than others. If a boy is reported to me for swearing at one of the domestic staff in the school dining hall, I am angry. Unlike the teaching staff, the domestic staff have no authority; they cannot hit back. Quite apart from other considerations, it is exactly what the ideal of good manners should prevent us from doing. Without making a mouthful of it, I put this point to the school. But some complaints reflect more on the complainant than on the boys. A bishop's chaplain wrote to complain that a group of boys coming out of the science block had not stepped aside to let him pass. I think he expected them to divide like the Red Sea at his approach. But why should they? If he had been an old lady that would have been different but I see no reason why boys, just because they are schoolboys, should be expected to step off the pavement for a clergyman. A brief spell in the gutter would have done his humility no harm.

Complaints about boys' bad manners are not infrequently linked to the use of bad language. You call the boys 'foul-mouthed'. They certainly use expletives that we did not. 'Bloody' is the most aggressive word I used at that age; they use 'fuck' and 'shit'. The bodily functions have replaced religion as the inspiration of our oaths. In their use of these words, the young ape the fashions of the adult world, particularly what the adult world tolerates in the media. My view of bad language is simple. If a boy's use of a swear-word causes embarrassment or offence it ought to be checked. It is a form of bad manners. But if he swears out loud when he is alone in the carpentry shop and hits his thumb with a hammer that is his business. Swear-words are neutral; they only become objectionable when someone is offended by them. The art of good manners (as well as of bad manners) is knowing who will be offended by what.

Given the example of the adult world, you are not going to stop the boys swearing. What you can do is to make them more circumspect and considerate about the time and place. The boy last term who told a canon in mufti to 'bugger off' had to learn that lesson, as do boys who swear on the games field. You may be surprised to hear that I have walked on the pitch during a first-eleven match to tell a boy that I would have him sent off if I heard him swearing again. But the boy was not from this school. He was a member of the visiting team. Our boys are neither more nor less foul-mouthed than those at other schools. When Mark goes to Sandhurst in the autumn he will find his fellow cadets very similar in their manners and language. When he meets his schoolfriends in five years' time, he will find most of them immaculately dressed, well-mannered and well-spoken.

It is not so much that you and I disagree on the importance of these things. It is just that having seen so many boys grow up, I know that the scruffy, ill-mannered and foul-mouthed adolescent is not a mirror of the man he will become.

Yours sincerely

JOHN RAE

4

LIVING DANGEROUSLY

Dear Mr and Mrs Carroll

Thank you for your phone call. What happened was this. James and two other boys of his year were reported to me by the police. They had been dodging in and out of the traffic in Victoria Street, seeing how close they could come to being hit by a car. The police had given the boys a verbal box on the ears; I reinforced this but did not give any punishment. I told them, 'It may seem exciting but it is just not worth the risk. You could have been killed or crippled for life.' And they gave the text-book response: 'We realize that now, sir.'

Yes, do talk to James about it but I wouldn't be heavy handed if I were you. What he did was foolish not immoral (though it could have caused an accident in which someone else was hurt), nor was it abnormal. What may look to us like lunatic behaviour has a certain logic to the adolescent. Dodging in and out of traffic both excites the senses and tests the nerve. 'How brave am I?' is an important question to a young man of fourteen.

But it *was* dangerous, a matter of split-second timing or a trial of wills between the driver and themselves. They stood in the middle of the road (so the police told me) facing the oncoming traffic and daring the drivers to run them down. It was a scene from the last reel of many a Western. Who will lose his nerve and draw his gun first? Do you remember that 'chicken run' in the James Dean film *Rebel Without a Cause*?

Dean and the leader of a hostile gang drive old cars towards the edge of a cliff: the first one to jump out is a chicken.

Headmasters are ambivalent towards this sort of behaviour. On one hand they must condemn it because they are responsible for the safety of their pupils. On the other, they know that for some adolescents the urge to take risks, to live dangerously, can be very strong and is bound to find expression in acts of bravado. If I punish a boy for living dangerously, the punishment is no more than is necessary to deter him from doing it again. From time to time I have warned the whole school against roof climbing, not because I think it is a major crime but because I want to cover myself and because I am afraid that in the dark on those rambling medieval roofs a false step could be fatal. There is only one thing more hazardous than a boy roof climbing at night and that is a master trying to catch him.

I had been to a City dinner and the brandy fumes still hung about. Footsteps on the roof. I climbed out of the window, still wearing my evening clothes, and up the iron fire-escape. Three dark figures were approaching across the roofs from the direction of the neighbouring boarding house. I hid behind the chimney stack. At the right moment I stepped out and said, 'Good evening, gentlemen.' (I confess to loving such moments. Chief Inspector Rae steps forward as the Great Train Robbers are about to divide the loot. 'Good evening, gentlemen!') If the boys were taken by surprise they did not show it. One of them muttered, 'Good evening.' I was on the point of telling them how dangerous this roof climbing was when I realized that the only person at risk of falling off was myself. They were young and sober. I was middle-aged and should have known that my roof climbing days were over. I sent them to bed, resolved to forget the incident. But in the morning I knew that I would have to warn them off. I could risk my life but not theirs.

The ambivalence in the headmaster's attitude is accentuated

47

in my case by an adolescence dominated by an almost compulsive desire to live dangerously. Middle-aged men enjoy exaggerating the escapades of their youth; like the daredevil boys they wish they had been, they cannot bear to be thought uninteresting. But this illustration from my youth is unadorned. I give it to you so that you can place James's escapade in its correct perspective.

When I was sixteen and at boarding school, I used to climb out of the dormitory window, which was about sixty feet from the ground. I had a series of party tricks to entertain and impress the other boys. I would lower myself and hang by one hand from the bottom of the metal window frame. I would climb round from one open window to the next; there were three windows together and the central one was always closed. I would pretend to slip and pull myself up again. I don't think my motivation was abnormal or complicated: I wanted the excitement and I wanted to be talked about. No doubt if the headmaster had known (neither he nor my parents ever did), he would have said: 'You could have been killed or crippled for life.' And I would have replied: 'I realize that now, sir.'

Can a fourteen-year-old focus on the reality of death? I do not think so. When like James or myself you take lunatic risks, part of your mind realizes the danger (otherwise where would be the excitement?) but another part suspends reality. The tension between reality and fantasy resolves itself in favour of the former but it can be a close-run thing. I can recall that, as I hung from the window, part of the thrill was to think about letting go. But the mind was always clear enough to come down on the side of reality.

There is nothing suicidal in the adolescent's attraction to danger. He doesn't want to die. To be 'half in love with easeful death' is a quite different state of mind prompted not by a desire to explore experience through taking risks but by a longing to escape from worldly cares. The adolescent is

48

gambling not escaping. The risks he takes are real but the odds on getting hurt are not so great. That is why roof climbing is such a favourite. There is enough danger, with the additional appeal that the activity is banned by the school authorities. One of the incidental advantages of boarding school is that it provides facilities for roof-climbing. I have sometimes wondered what I would have done for excitement if I had remained at home at a day school in the suburbs of London. No roofs, no high windows, no captive audience . . . I might well have turned to crime.

How can a school contain this fascination with danger and see its adolescents through to an age when they can calculate more rationally the risks they want to take?

Two hundred years ago the problem seems to have been solved by allowing the boys so much freedom that there was danger enough and to spare. If you read *Boys Together*, John Chandos's book about the old public schools, you will be amazed by the wild, exuberant lives of the eighteenth-century public schoolboys – the bare-knuckle fights to the death, the mob violence, the rebellions, the attacks on gamekeepers, the stoning of animals, the drunken escapades. How mild and inoffensive James's traffic dodging appears in comparison! The almost total freedom enjoyed by these eighteenth-century boys outside the classroom would be regarded as the height of permissiveness today. In the nineteenth and early twentieth centuries, the schools reacted against the earlier anarchy and organized the boys, hoping to channel their love of danger and violence into competitive sport. Now, in the late twentieth century, the pendulum has swung back towards freedom for the boys, but only so far. Optimists think the schools now strike a good balance between freedom and organization. Pessimists think we have the worst of both worlds: not enough freedom to let the boys enjoy the excitement of the jungle; not enough organization to keep boredom at bay.

Boredom is one of the great enemies for the adolescent not

so much because he has nothing to do but because he cannot settle to anything. He is both restless and becalmed. He is impatient for manhood but there is nothing he can do to hasten the process. Small wonder that he should try to inject some excitement into the dog-days. Headmasters are aware of the dangers of boredom and of the need to provide opportunities for taking risks. Competitive sport still fulfils its function, though less effectively than in the past; clubs and societies stimulate interests and occupy time; community service encourages more sober reflection (nothing like a geriatric ward for bringing the madcap down to earth); and climbing in Snowdonia makes a rather dull but acceptable alternative to climbing on the headmaster's roof.

But precisely because these activities are approved by the adult world, there will always be some boys who are determined to take their risks in their own way. The headmaster's job is to do all he can to protect the adolescents from themselves while keeping his sense of proportion. The roof-climbers and the traffic-dodgers are not wicked, nor are they corrupting others. They are just growing up.

Is there something wrong with the adolescent who shows no inclination to live dangerously? I think not. The extraordinary diversity of human nature seems to allow for any number of successful routes through adolescence. But I gave a silent cheer when I heard that an otherwise impeccably behaved young man had been caught with other boys climbing at night on the scaffolding on the south face of the Abbey. He was sixteen, the only child of rather elderly parents, always immaculate in the presentation of himself and his work. He was happier in the company of adults than with his rowdy contemporaries.

The boys were caught by the Abbey security staff. I saw them before school the following morning. Three of them were old hands who did their best to look contrite. The other boy could hardly lift his eyes from the ground. He was overcome with shame. How could I tell him that I was delighted he had gone along? His parents hastened to see me. They were shocked: their son had never done anything wrong before at school or at home. I did my best to explain to them that it was not altogether a bad thing that their son had broken the perfect pattern of his growing up. They did not or could not see it that way. The boy is now in his twenties, a lawyer in the City. I see him from time to time. He is already elderly in his manner. Perhaps, with the exception of that brief moment on the scaffolding, he was never young.

I hope this letter helps you to put James's escapade in perspective. He is still only fourteen, he still wants to know the answer to the question, 'How brave am I?' What you and I must do is to try to ensure that in finding that answer he does not take risks that are unnecessary or unpredictable.

Yours sincerely

JOHN RAE

5

LYING

Dear Mrs Roach

Are you not partly to blame? I do not think parents should trap their children into lying. If you knew that Rupert did not get back from the Drummonds' party until three in the morning, why did you ask him at breakfast in front of the whole family what time he went to bed? You say this is the first time he has deliberately deceived you. That may be true but there is a sense in which you also deceived him. By asking the question you implied that you did not know the answer. You misled him into thinking that he could get away with disobeying your edict that he must be home by midnight. Why didn't you get him on his own and say, 'Look, I told you to be home at midnight but I heard you coming in at three. What happened?'

I don't condone Rupert's lie but I don't approve of your approach either. Jesuit inquisitors and Gestapo officers were trained to trick their prisoners into lying. Rupert isn't your prisoner, he's your sixteen-year-old son and he isn't on trial. Surely you should encourage him to tell the truth, not tempt him to lie. By now he will probably have worked out that you knew all along and he will be angry and resentful that he fell into your trap.

I would not recommend confronting him about it. Not now. Try to find some time together when he is at home this weekend so that if he wants to he can say, 'Actually I came home at three after the party. I'm sorry I lied to you.' If he does, please don't play the deeply hurt mother – 'I've always trusted you to tell me the truth ever since you were a child.' Nothing is more calculated to make a boy his age want to rush for the door. If he apologizes, so should you. Admit that you knew and say you're sorry you pretended you didn't.

I hope he wants to tell you the truth but don't bank on it. He may justify that deliberate lie by telling himself that you were wrong to ask him. He may be blaming the whole episode on what he sees as your attempts to treat him as a child. *I* think you were right to set a time for his return and I doubt whether Rupert objected to it or intended to be so late, but your trap and his lie have turned a routine family hiccup into a struggle between your colonial power and his liberation movement. So tread carefully. Parents need considerable political finesse if they are to retain the respect of their offspring after the struggle for independence is over.

Yours sincerely

JOHN RAE

Dear Dr Rae

I found your letter unhelpful and in some respects offensive. A lie is a lie, yet you apparently believe that it is I who should feel guilty. I did not deceive Rupert. I asked him a straight-forward question and he told me a deliberate lie. If you cannot see that he is wrong, are you fit to be responsible for the education of other people's children? Truthfulness is at the heart of all moral teaching. If you, as headmaster, fudge this issue, your pupils cannot be blamed for regarding honesty as a matter of convenience rather than principle. I know that Victorian values are out of fashion but I cannot imagine one of the great Victorian headmasters, such as Dr Arnold, having any doubts whatsoever about the seriousness of telling a lie, particularly to one's parents. Your special pleading on Rupert's behalf is typical of the liberal intellectual's reluctance to make a clear distinction between right and wrong. I could accept your advice more readily if I believed that you practised what you preached. But I have often heard the boys talking about you when Rupert has a group home for the weekend and I can assure you that one thing they particularly dislike about you is the way you frighten boys into confessing by threatening to expel them if they tell you a lie. I suggest you look at your own inquisitorial methods before criticizing those used by parents.

Yours sincerely

Amanda Roach

*   *   *

Dear Mrs Roach

I *am* unfit to be a headmaster if I fail to encourage a respect for truth or if I use unscrupulous methods to extract confessions. I will defend myself against those charges but first I must make clear my attitude to your treatment of Rupert.

I am not going to lie to you and say I think there has been a misunderstanding. You understand me well enough but you refuse to recognize that your 'straightforward' question was not straightforward at all since you knew the answer. It was a trap or, if you prefer, a test. You wanted to check whether Rupert was still the George Washington you remembered. I don't think what you did was immoral; I just think it was devious. That doesn't make Rupert's lie any less wrong but it does suggest how it could have been avoided.

We are not required, are we, to set our children moral tests? As parents, not only are our emotions engaged but our motives are not as unselfish as we like to think. When a mother sets a truth trap for her son, she may think she is acting entirely in the interests of his moral development, but is there not also a selfish desire to confirm her power over him? If fathers are less inclined these days to set moral traps for their offspring it is not because they have grown wiser or kinder but because they find the prospect of a confrontation disagreeable, particularly at the breakfast table. They prefer to say, as I know having used the formula on many occasions, 'I will have a word with him about it later,' an undertaking that as often as not is postponed or forgotten.

Rupert seldom sees his father and when he does it is unlikely that morality is high on the agenda. The burden of your son's moral education falls on you and on me. We should at least understand one another's position.

I am not equivocal on the question of lying but I differ from the great Victorian headmasters in this respect: they regarded lying as evil in its highest form, so much so that their response to it could be literally uncontrollable. You mention Dr Arnold. On one occasion he thrashed a young boy for eighteen strokes because he believed the boy had lied to him, only to discover afterwards that he had been telling the truth all along. What can have driven such a man to this excess? It was partly a noble obsession with truth at all costs, truthfulness as the key to godliness and the pursuit of truth as the goal of learning. But it was partly an inability or unwillingness to recognize that boys together have a different moral code. There are times when a boy sees it as his duty to lie to authority. His loyalty to his contemporaries requires it and that loyalty overrides all other considerations.

You may not like my inquisitorial methods but I have never asked or expected a boy to betray his friends or his enemies. A headmaster must respect the code of the school-boy mafia unless the crime he is investigating is too serious to be protected by *omertà*, the code of silence. Times change and so do the activities that boys are prepared to protect. Not long ago two boys came to see me of their own accord to report a particularly vicious bully. Thirty years ago that would not have happened. But even today boys will not 'finger' one of their own number in cases that you and I would regard as serious, such as those involving stealing or drugs. It is of course partly because the more serious offences carry the probability of expulsion; I have to accept that draconian punishments strengthen the taboo against co-operation with the authorities. There is nothing new in this. The severity of Victorian headmasters' floggings prompted Charles Kingsley to write, 'The boy learns not to fear sin but the punishment of it, and thus he learns to lie.'

This talk of the mafia makes the schoolboy world sound more sinister than it is. But the Sicilian word *omertà* is not altogether ill chosen. It means more than keeping silent. There is also a sense that manliness (ironically a word used by Victorian headmasters in quite a different sense) requires you to solve your own problems without going to the authorities. That code, though it is used by organizations such as the mafia and the IRA, is not dishonourable when used by schoolboys and as far as I can tell has always existed among them.

Headmasters such as Dr Arnold refused to see anything honourable in it. Arnold expelled a boy (the elder brother of Thomas Hughes who wrote *Tom Brown's Schooldays*) for failing to give him the names of boys who had misbehaved on Guy Fawkes' night. I think that was immoral. Truthfulness is a virtue that no headmaster can fail to uphold but he must temper his eagerness to instil it in his pupils with an understanding of the pressures that operate in the schoolboy underworld. There is, however, a form of lying that I hate with as much passion as the Victorian headmasters. I am talking about the lies that enable people to do evil things with a clear conscience. If religious people seem particularly prone to lie in this way, they certainly do not have the copyright. Historical examples will occur to you, particularly during periods of religious persecution but they are only an extreme form of a more domestic phenomenon.

In my first year here the parents of a new boy divorced in a way that created maximum bitterness between them. Father had gone to live with a younger woman. Mother was vengeful and determined to turn their only child, Adrian, against his father. She was a religious woman, an evangelical Christian and she used the bible to prove to Adrian that his father would burn in hell. What made her method so abhorrent – I heard all this from Adrian himself many years later – was that she told her son that while she as a Christian could forgive her husband, God could never do so. She put on a saintly de-meanour while brainwashing her son with a hatred of his father that lasted until Adrian was in his early twenties. She told friends that it was her moral duty to see that Adrian had no doubts about the sinfulness of adultery. At thirteen he was an easy victim. Mother had custody and although father was given 'reasonable access', Adrian refused to see him. It is not the mother's anger and desire to hurt her husband that provokes me. Who wouldn't feel those emotions? It is the lie she told herself and others about her true motives. Filling her son with hatred for his father was bad enough but to pretend that she was acting from the highest religious motives was a lie that I would find it very hard to forgive.

Compared with that mother's vindictive dishonesty, Rupert's answer to your question has all the innocence of a spontaneous lie. It was wrong but it had an amateurishness about it that should make it easier to forgive. The professional deceiver seldom needs to tell such a blatant lie.

I have left till last your swipe at my way of obtaining con-fessions from boys. It stung because there is truth in it. I *have* said to boys that the one thing they must not do is to tell a lie to the headmaster; I have never said that they would be expelled for doing so, though I think the threat was implied. The boy who is guilty of a serious offence is caught in a Catch

22. If he confesses he is likely to be expelled. If he lies and the lie is detected he is certain to be expelled. Heads I win, tails you lose. There is something distasteful (one might put it more strongly) about this approach. I would never use it to pressure a boy into giving evidence against another, only against himself and only in serious cases involving drugs or bullying. I think that the public good authorizes a degree of ruthlessness that in less serious cases would be regarded as unfair, if not immoral.

As a historian, I am bound to say that that sounds like a Machiavellian ruler justifying his ruthless suppression of those who challenge his authority. Yet I still believe that my approach, which you say the boys so much dislike, is necessary. I may have other motives, some of which I do not recognize, but I know that one conscious motive is a desire to prevent other boys from getting into serious trouble. An investigation that leads nowhere, especially when the school knows the individual is guilty, is not a good deterrent.

What your letter has made me realize is that my criticism of the Victorian headmasters is somewhat hypocritical. When I say to a boy, 'At all costs, do not lie to me,' I am using, not encouraging truthfulness. Just like my Victorian predecessors I am imposing my interpretation of what it means to be truthful and just like them I justify it by reference to the public good. They wanted to root out vice but so do I. It is only the definition of what is vicious that has shifted. Perhaps we all – headmasters and parents – are too prone to use our values as a means of controlling the young instead of demonstrating by the way we live that the values have real importance for us.

I am sorry if my first letter gave offence. I have learnt something from our exchange though I am still puzzled by the strength of feeling your question to Rupert provoked in me. Some long-forgotten conflict of growing up, no doubt. But my advice holds good. Let Rupert tell you that he lied;

that is probably what he wants to do, not because he is an angel (or even genuinely sorry) but because he owes it to you and wants to clear his overdraft. But leave the initiative to him. I wouldn't drop hints or try to lead him to the point of confession. An adolescent boy can be very sensitive to every nuance of his mother's relationship with him, particularly any suggestion that she wants to extend her lease on his emotions.

Yours sincerely

JOHN RAE

6

STEALING

Dear Mr and Mrs Byron

When we last spoke you said that a good school ought to be able to contain adolescent rebellions without resorting to expulsion. The headmaster – in your metaphor – is the world heavyweight champion; he doesn't have to knock out every novice to prove his point.

I don't disagree with that. But stealing isn't adolescent rebellion. It may be a daredevil act that does not merit expulsion. But more often than not it is a crime. Why call it by any other name?

I have expelled the two fifteen-year-old boys. You will think that harsh but I think it necessary. There is too much stealing of property and money in all types of school and the well-known boys' independent schools are no exception.

This was a particularly bad case. They broke into another boy's box and stole £55 in cash. The box was like an old-fashioned tuck box, wooden but reinforced with metal and padlocked. The thieves could not break the padlock so they used a commando knife to split the wood. I am surprised no one heard them but it was a games afternoon and the house was almost deserted. Because they were off games (for no good reason it turned out, the house matron being conned into giving them a chit) they fell under suspicion at once. When questioned by the housemaster, each appeared to be trying to cast suspicion on the other: it was a carefully rehearsed performance. The accusation and counter-accusation, far from incriminating them, seemed to cast doubt on both their stories so the housemaster, exhausted and confused, almost eliminated them from his enquiries. Almost but not quite. He consulted his housemonitors. The senior boys were in no doubt that the two were guilty. The whole house was watching the housemaster's inability to pin the crime on the two boys with a mixture of cynicism and incredulity. His own position, the monitors implied, would be undermined if the boys got away with it.

It is a mistake to underestimate the cunning of boys. They lie with disarming facility. They also know when it is prudent to tell the truth. When adults advise that 'honesty is the best policy', the schoolboy takes the advice literally; there comes a time when honesty is indeed the best policy but *it is a policy*, not a moral choice. We should not be surprised by this. The instinct for survival is at its most animal when we are young; social and moral obligations domesticate the instinct as we mature, though in moments of danger, it's true, untamed nature will flare out again.

The boys in this case went on lying until it was politic to tell the truth. Their housemaster asked me to see them. He was sure they were guilty but their ingenious technique of mutual accusation made it difficult to pin the theft on either of them. I saw them first individually and then together. I, too, thought it probable that they were guilty but I was no more successful in finding any proof. I could not expel them just because 'everybody knows that they did it', nor would public opinion make life difficult for them. Pupils do not regard thieving as part of the traditional battle of wits against authority, but they reckon it is authority's job to bring the thieves to justice.

If the boys had stuck to their stories there would have been nothing I could have done. There was no real evidence against them: no one had seen them entering or leaving the other boy's study; in their own study there was no sign of the stolen money or of the commando knife; they were not short of cash; they had their own bank accounts and a monthly allowance from their parents that should have comfortably provided for their needs. They were in the clear. Their mistake was to overplay their hand. The mutual accusations, hiding the real lies in a confusing pattern of false ones, would have been a clever device if they had needed to discredit evidence against them. As it was, it only served to trap them. They could not remember exactly what lies they had told their housemaster and had not reckoned on him making detailed notes of the conversations. When I pointed out inconsistencies they claimed the housemaster was deliberately cooking the evidence in order to pin the theft on them. But, they added, they did not blame him. They realized that he was under pressure from the senior boys in the house; they were very understanding.

The interrogation was a long business. Fifteen-year-olds with something to hide have considerable stamina. There were times when I felt like dropping the whole thing – after all, they were only fifteen, there was a limit to the amount of pressure it was fair for me to place upon them. Were they really so wicked that I had to follow through to what would certainly be a bitter end? What made me continue? Was it a genuine desire that criminals should be identified and punished, or fear that if I did not discover the truth my own credibility would be undermined?

In this case the bitter end came in an unexpected way. I had sent the two boys away and told them to come back and see me at the end of prep. I wanted them to have a chance to talk it over and I hoped (without much confidence) that they would return ready to confess. They did, but not in the terms I had anticipated. They came to my study at nine o'clock and sat together on the sofa. I asked them if they had anything further to say. One of them answered in the following terms.

They were very sorry for the trouble they had caused; they had been lying all along. They realized that there was no real evidence against them and that without their confessions I could not expel them. Nevertheless they had decided that it was in the interests of the school to have the matter cleared up. They wished to make a full confession and to throw themselves on my mercy.

They were young and had not been in serious trouble before. Why not accept their change of heart as genuine and give them a second chance? I had good reasons for not doing so. The school's position on stealing had been made clear on a number of occasions both by my explicit warnings at assembly and by the severity of the punishments when thieves were caught. Yet these two boys planned and carried out a major theft. It was not a spur-of-the-moment yielding to temptation, the sort of opportunist crime that accounts for many thefts in schools. It was premeditated to the extent that the false trail of lies had also been prepared. If I allowed them to remain, the school would conclude that stealing had been taken off the list of serious offences; and the consequences of that would be that many more boys would be tempted into trouble. They had to be expelled.

Why did they become thieves? The reasons for schoolboy stealing are not difficult to understand. Boys steal because they want to possess something that is not theirs or because they enjoy the excitement of taking a risk. I believe it is exceptional for there to be a deeper explanation. I accept that if a middle-aged woman steals from a supermarket her action may be interpreted as a cry for help or attention. That could also be true of a schoolboy thief, neglected by his parents, but it is rare. Boys steal for greed and for kicks; to attribute such commonplace human motives to psychological disturbance confuses the issue unnecessarily, and prevents the individual concerned from facing up to the moral question of what is right and wrong behaviour.

I was punished for stealing at school. I was eleven and at a preparatory boarding school. War-time rationing meant that chocolate and sweets were hard to come by. A gang of about eight boys, led by two thirteen-year-olds, planned and executed efficient 'raids' on the local confectioners. The gang operated the well-established principle that if the shop-keeper's attention was concentrated on a group of boys clamouring to be served, he would not see the others filling their pockets. I only took part in one raid, not because I had qualms, but because soon after I was recruited the operation was blown. Someone – I assume – had grassed.

I cannot remember how I was recruited or exactly why I agreed to join. I imagine that there was an element of wanting to 'keep in with the boys'. But knowing myself I am sure that the excitement was the chief attraction. For a young boy during the war it had all the thrill of a commando raid. I cannot have been unaware of the moral implications. I knew stealing was wrong. In 1942 moral distinctions were clear cut and my parents' non-conformist upbringing meant that their children were left in no doubt that dishonesty of any sort was unacceptable. It interests me now to note that my parents' sensible morality was not proof against the pressure of my contemporaries and the lure of danger.

We were all beaten by the headmaster. We went in one by one. The senior master had a list with the number of strokes beside each name: six for the leaders, four for the other ranks. 'Rae four,' he announced as I stepped forward. It was like a prize-giving.

This was not the only punishment. We were told to write to our parents telling them what had happened. It is a familiar headmaster's tactic. Parents have to know. Better their son should have a chance to break the bad news. And the drafting of the letter calls for an early exercise of diplomatic skills. A boy cannot learn too soon the art of presenting his lapses from grace in the least unfavourable light. I started the letter by saying that some boys had been caught stealing. Then – and I remember the phrase exactly – I went on: 'Fortunately, I only took one bar of chocolate.' My mother was not misled: stealing was a matter of principle, not degree. She replied: 'Promise me that you will never do such a thing again.' I did and I didn't.

I do not think the two boys I have expelled stole for kicks. It was common knowledge that the victim had a large sum of cash and I suspect the thieves could not resist the opportunity of having extra money to spend. (I asked the victim why he kept such a large sum in his room instead of handing it in to the house bank. He replied that he found it intolerable to have to explain to his housemaster why he needed the money every time he made a withdrawal.) If greed was the motive, it was in the exact sense of covetousness. They had money. They wanted more. For drink or drugs or cigarettes? Probably not. My guess would be records or tickets for this or that pop concert. Whatever it was the moral safety mechanism did not operate. I can only assume that the desire for more spending power was too strong.

I saw both sets of parents this morning. They were shocked and baffled. They were also critical of the school. Their sons had never stolen anything in their lives before. (I did not point out that all we could say was that they had never been caught.) One of the fathers was a regular soldier. He commanded a regiment. As I explained the reasons for his son's expulsion, he kept interjecting: 'There are no bad soldiers, Headmaster, only bad officers.' It did not seem to have occurred to him that in relation to his own son he might be the bad officer.

It is hard for parents to know how to react. Because they are emotionally involved they find it difficult to get the tone and emphasis right. One of the disadvantages of boarding school is that this emotion may have to be expressed in a letter or postponed. You cannot easily express your feelings to your son on the stairs outside the headmaster's study or in the car parked outside or in the hotel lounge to which you retreat. My father did not see me until I returned home at the end of that term. For several weeks he referred to me within the family as 'Thievey John', as though his embarrassment and mine would disappear with everyday use. He was a kind man. Perhaps he just could not help himself. It would have been so much easier for him if he had been able to be angry with me at the time.

The ideal parental response would not exclude anger or an unequivocal condemnation of stealing, but both would be expressed in the context of parental love. I doubt whether the parents of the two boys I expelled will approach that ideal. They are too anxious to place the blame on the school. When they left, it was with sharp words to me about the need to improve its moral climate.

How much is the school to blame? Home and parents are a more important influence but the school also communicates values. If a school takes the line (as some do) that it cannot prevent thefts and that responsibility for the security of property rests with the owner, the pupils will conclude that stealing, like bad weather, is an inconvenient fact of life rather than a question of right and wrong behaviour. But it *is* a question of right and wrong and the school must not let the moral argument go by default. It is the headmaster's job to make the moral case, both explicitly in what he says to the assembled school and implicitly in how he reacts to the stealing that occurs. However much he may recoil from the public exposition of morality, he must not fail in this. He cannot plead the moral ambiguity of the times or claim that it was so much easier for Dr Arnold. It wasn't. When Arnold was at Rugby in the second quarter of the nineteenth century, the borderline between crime and schoolboy peccadillo could be just as difficult to discern as it is today, and Arnold's definition was often highly unpopular with the boys. His authority was never more seriously threatened than when he expelled six boys, including some of the 'heroes' of the school, for poaching fish. The whole school was against him and his senior boys refused to co-operate in identifying the guilty.

Arnold was not only concerned with morality. He was worried about the school's reputation. A similar anxiety about reputation makes today's headmasters reluctant to discuss stealing in their schools. Some deny that it occurs at all. Others are prepared to admit that 'a certain amount of pilfering goes on'. If I were a parent, I should be suspicious of a headmaster who talks about pilfering. If he means stealing, why doesn't he call it by its proper name?

Stealing is commonplace in all types of school: independent and maintained, boys' and girls', primary and secondary. Thieving crosses the barriers of class, sex and age. The heads of independent schools, who operate in the market place, are understandably sensitive on this issue. They are angry at any suggestion that a fee-paying school with a Christian foundation might share the problem of thieving with the local comprehensive. At the Annual Meeting of the Headmasters' Conference in Edinburgh in 1980, there was a public session on 'Values in our Schools'. The debate seemed to me to be adopting an increasingly self-congratulatory tone. How lucky we are to have our Christian traditions; how hard it must be for our colleagues in the comprehensives. This bland hypocrisy provoked my intervention. I stood up to say that I did not think there was a school in the conference where a boy could leave a pocket calculator lying around and be sure that it would still be there five minutes later. My fellow headmasters were furious. How dare I make sweeping allegations of dishonesty? One headmaster was particularly incensed. He knew for a fact that there was no stealing in his school. My comment was outrageous. It *was* outrageous if you take the view that the public image is paramount. But I received letters from many parents saying that they were glad that the problem had been brought into the open: they knew from their own children that stealing was a common enough occurrence.

Stealing is not a new problem in schools. What has changed is that to the time-honoured schoolboy practice of 'borrowing' pens, books and games clothes has been added an element of straightforward crime. Boys who were found in possession of someone else's books were not regarded as criminals by their peers or by the school authorities. But the boy who stole money was. The latter was a real thief as distinct from a naughty schoolboy. It is real thieving that has increased. The taboo against stealing money and valuable personal items, such as watches, seems to have been eroded. There is of course more money around but that alone cannot account for the shift from schoolboy naughtiness to schoolboy crime.

I think the increase in schoolboy thieving reflects a lowering of the moral threshold of this issue in our society. I mean by this that, particularly in the case of money, people feel less inhibited than they used to do about taking or keeping what is not theirs. Much of the dishonesty is of a passive kind: if the conductor fails to ask for my fare, that is his fault; if the check-out girl gives me too much change, that is her fault; if a stranger drops a £10 note in the street, so much the worse for him. Finding the conductor, returning the excess change, handing the note to the police, would be regarded as quixotic, if not positively stupid. You may think these are trivial matters but I am trying to establish a shift in the climate of opinion. What would once have caused some heart searching at least, is now regarded as common sense.

On a more serious level, the number of indictable offences of shoplifting known to the police rose steadily during the Seventies and Eighties; and in case you think that this is another illustration of lack of discipline among the young – the usual middle-aged explanation – only 16 per cent of those charged were under the age of seventeen. It is adult dishonesty that is on the increase. Libraries, particularly at universities, now install elaborate security measures to prevent the stealing of books. Thefts from offices by employees rose by 20 per cent in 1978 alone. There is more evidence but that should suffice.

Stealing has been downgraded in the calendar of crimes. Public figures, including some MPs, claim that people found with goods for which they have not paid are not dishonest but victims, tempted unfairly by attractive and accessible shop displays. In the same way, headmasters sometimes apportion blame equally between owner and thief by saying of the former: 'It's just as much his fault for leaving money lying around.' There is a general unwillingness to call a thief a thief. My father may have gone about it the wrong way but at least I was left in no doubt that what I had done was wrong. Today's euphemisms and evasions must leave the young in some confusion.

None of which relieves parents and headmasters of the responsibility of driving home the moral argument against stealing. If they don't, who will?

But is expulsion the right punishment? I think there is a distinction between thefts that take on the nature of crimes and those that retain the character of schoolboy naughtiness. The distinction is not always easy to make. I have given a second chance to a boy whose theft was off the cuff and small in scale; I have not given a second chance where the theft was on a significant scale and clearly premeditated. It is a rough-and-ready guide but one which the other pupils understand. It also sustains the moral argument without depopulating the school. Good heavens, if every pupil who ever took anything that did not belong to him was expelled, our schools would be half empty.

Yours sincerely

JOHN RAE

7

BULLYING

Dear Mark and Jane

I can imagine how you feel and I'm sure you can imagine how I feel. I am so very sorry it should have happened at all but especially that it should have happened to Toby. You sent him here because we were friends, and although you knew that I could not protect him from all the hard knocks, you trusted me to run the sort of school where serious bullying would not occur. How complacent I was. I believed that bullying, though not eradicated altogether, was so rare that parents had little to fear on that score.

You are angry that Toby should have been driven to run away, though your letter does not show it; only sadness and a question: 'Where do we go from here?' Your other question, though unspoken, is not unheard. 'Why did the school allow this to happen?'

The purpose of this letter is to answer both your questions.

You say that Toby has not told you exactly what happened. I must tell you though you will not thank me for it. The housemaster and I have questioned the four boys responsible and I do not think there is any doubt about the facts.

Toby was the only new boy in his house. As you know, that is unusual but not unknown at the start of the spring term. You will remember that we spoke about the possible problems of his settling in when it was decided to postpone his entry from September. The bullies were the four other boys in his dormitory. They are all about Toby's age – one is fourteen but the others are, like him, still thirteen – and had all joined the school in September. Two had been at the same prep school as Toby. When I spoke to the prep school headmaster yesterday, he told me that your son had had some trouble with these two boys in the past, though nothing was said about this when Toby came here. If you or I had known, we would have thought twice about putting him in the same house as them. That excuses nothing but it might help to explain why this happened.

The four boys picked on Toby because he was alone. The instigator and ringleader was Simon R—— (I do not suppose the name means anything to you). He was one of the two boys who was at prep school with Toby. He is big for his age and as physically developed as a boy of fifteen or sixteen. It was he who invented the 'house tradition' of an initiation ceremony for new boys. As all the boys were in the same dormitory there was no problem finding an opportunity. After lights out that Friday, they told Toby to take off his pyjamas. Three of them held him face down on his bed while Simon R—— forced a cricket stump up his anus. It was, needless to say, extremely painful and degrading for Toby. The homosexual overtones are obvious but the motive was surely cruelty. We tend to forget, until something like this happens, how much we enjoy other people's suffering.

When they told Toby that another humiliating ceremony was to take place on the two following Friday nights, he decided to run away. You can understand why he refused to tell you what the boys had done to him. I have had to tell you but I think you should keep it to yourself. If Toby learns that you know what happened, his sense of shame and humiliation will be intensified. Let him tell you if he wants to but my guess is he never will. That is not necessarily bad for him. We are so keen on talking over our problems these days that we overlook the value of having to work them out for ourselves. Your instinct will be to bring the problem out into the open; mine is to let Toby wrestle with it inside himself. Parents, like anyone else whose role is not clearly defined, want to be seen to be doing something. Try to let him know that you are ready to listen if he wants to tell you but that you are not pressing. And for God's sake, act together. I'm sorry if that sounds rude but I have known too many parents who have tried to exploit this sort of situation to score points in the marital conflict. 'You can tell me, dear, and I promise not to tell your father because he wouldn't really understand, would he?'

You can also understand why Toby is so adamant that he will not come back to school. Yet if it is at all possible, that is what you and I have got to persuade him to do. I do not think he will have any more trouble from the three boys who are still here. As you know, I have expelled the ringleader. I had to weigh the risk of repercussions that would further isolate Toby, against the need to punish deliberate cruelty and to be seen to take a stand against bullying. You feared that by doing this I was ensuring that the whole school would know exactly what had happened but the whole school was bound to know anyway. The grapevine is efficient and unstoppable. Toby's fear is not that he will be bullied again but that for the rest of his schooldays he will be a marked man: 'Isn't that the boy who . . . ?' It is easy for me to say that the other boys will forget much sooner than he imagines and that it will not help his struggle for maturity if he decides that he cannot face the prospect of returning. I am not sure that at thirteen I could have faced it. It might help if he knew that public opinion in the school is very hostile towards the four boys. The school monitors and some members of the common room think that they all should have been expelled. If Toby does come back he will not find the community unsympathetic. Easily said. He still has to face alone the first class, the first lunch in the house, the first night with new dormitory companions. Those moments won't be easy but they will pass.

Can bullying be prevented? Any headmaster who gives such an assurance is lying. He cannot control every moment of his pupils' lives. What he hopes to achieve is a public opinion in the school that condemns bullying and a pastoral structure that is sensitive enough to pick up the first signs of trouble. In Toby's case, neither safeguard was good enough. Public opinion clearly did nothing to deter the four boys. On the pastoral side, the housemaster does not ask enough of his house monitors. I am not passing the buck, just expressing a view. There was a house monitor in the next room but he says he heard nothing. Perhaps there was nothing to hear. All the same, I find it hard to believe that a housemaster who was really in touch with his house would have failed to spot a potential bully in Simon K—. But I knew Toby well and K— well enough; I should have given more thought to the possible dangers of placing Toby in that house. We might have prevented the incident if we had all been a bit more efficient.

It might help you, particularly in talking to Toby, if I tell you what my experience of bullying has been. I was not bullied at school. I had an older brother who went on ahead, drawing the enemies' fire and building for himself a reputation as a fierce fighter. I was safe in his wake. By the time I was Toby's age I could look after myself. I was physically strong enough to deter my contemporaries and aggressive enough in a somewhat unpredictable way (a defensive technique that a number of boys adopt) to make the bigger boys wary. They turned their attention to easier prey.

The easier prey were often boys who seemed to be natural victims. I use that phrase with caution because it sounds like the argument that some women invite rape. But there is something about the personality, the appearance, the circumstances of some boys that attracts bullies. In some cases that 'something' is obvious: too easily provoked by teasing, for example. In other cases, the explanation is more complex but it usually amounts to a mismatch between the individual and his contemporaries.

Toby was bullied at his prep school and again here. Does that mean that he is one of the natural victims? I think not. That is not just to persuade you that he should return. Toby is shy, it is true, but he has a likeable personality and gets on well with the other boys of his age despite the evidence of this incident. I think he has been the victim of malice and of our mismanagement, not of any mismatch between himself and the boys around him.

If you are not convinced, let me tell you about a boy whose personality clearly was a mismatch. He was Toby's age and was being persistently teased in class, in break and in the house. If you had met him, you would have known at once why this was happening. His appearance and his manner set him apart from the other boys, not in a way that they could accept, like foreignness or physical disability, but in a way that seemed almost to mock them. He was an only child and had been much pampered at home and, as is sometimes the way with only children, had spent more time with adults than with his contemporaries. His figure was chubby, his voice unbroken but his gestures and language were sophisticated, elaborate and affected. He cried out to be teased and the hounds set upon him from his first day at the school. It was the sort of verbal bullying that is difficult to prevent unless the teacher is quick-witted and experienced. The housemaster was alerted and spoke to all the teachers but the teasing continued both in and out of class. The other boys became addicted to it as a way of making their own lives more entertaining. The victim did not break down or retaliate. He did just what you or I might have advised him to do: he treated his persecutors with contempt. But his aloofness spurred them on. Maybe it wasn't convincing enough; maybe it only served to whet their appetite for the kill. One day he was passed a note in class. He unfolded the paper and read: 'Tell us, —, what does "fuck" mean?'

For some reason that was the breaking point. He started to cry. The master asked him what was the matter but the boy ran out of the room. The hounds had won. His parents arranged for him to go to another independent school but almost at once, the same pattern of teasing began. He stuck it for the best part of a term and then left. He went to a small tutorial college but was not happy there. His problem all along was that he was unboyish in his manner and outlook while childish in his physical development. His contemporaries recognized an outsider and treated him as one.

I am all too familiar with the sense of impotent rage that a parent feels when he learns that his son or daughter is being bullied at school. I have daydreamed of going to the school to teach the bullies a lesson. Any parent who has not had that daydream is fortunate indeed. We had a parent once who turned the daydream into reality. He was a Spanish nobleman who had held senior rank in the Spanish army and was now a businessman in London. When he learnt that his son was being bullied, he left his office at once and came to the school. It was the mid-morning break. He found his son and demanded that he point out the bully. The bully was identified and the hidalgo took him on one side. The message was in broken English but unmistakable. 'You touch my son again and I deal with you. I no joke; is true!' The bully told his own father who complained to me of the Spaniard's 'outrageous behaviour'. I should have told him to get lost but, coward or diplomat that I was, I agreed to pass on the complaint. The Spanish nobleman reacted in character: he challenged the English shipping broker to a duel. It didn't happen, of course, but the Spanish boy was never bullied again. His father had taken the direct action that we all dream of.

You were right not to send Toby back straight away. At a crisis, a child needs assurance of his parents' love more than anything else. The 'make-a-man-of-him' approach can have damaging results. There was a case at another school where a young boy who was being bullied implored his father to take him away. His father refused: his son had to learn to stand on his own feet. Unable to bear it any longer, the boy rang home to make a last plea. He did not have enough money and reversed the charges. He heard the operator ask his father, 'I have a call from a — call-box. Will you pay for the call?' And then his father's unyielding reply, 'No, certainly not.' The boy returned to school and tried to take his own life. If school and home turn against you, there is nowhere else to go. Mercifully, he was found in time. His father – I am told – was more embarrassed than angry. What would the neighbours say?

Toby knows you are on his side. You can, and I think you should now press him to return to school. Because he is assured of your love there is no risk in your being firm with him. I wouldn't have a long debate about it if I were you; just assume he is coming back and act accordingly. That will make it easier for him to dismiss the alternatives.

Yours sincerely

JOHN RAE

(Toby came back to school the day his father received my letter. He just turned up and slipped back into school routine. When I asked his father about it, he told me that Toby's change of heart had occurred without any prompting from his parents. They were still reading my letter when he came into the kitchen and said, 'I'm going back now, can you give me a lift?' What had happened was that one of his schoolfellows had telephoned to say that 'people' wanted him to come back. That was all it needed, an assurance from a fellow soldier in the front line. The assurances of parents and headmasters can never have that authority.

That is all ten years ago now. Toby finished his school career in style, as a school monitor and as an actor whose performance as Macbeth had astonishing power and maturity. He went to Durham University. By chance, Simon K— went to Durham in the same year. His father had sent him to the local comprehensive school 'as a punishment'. Expressed in those terms, it could have been a formula for disaster but the staff at the school handled him well. At Durham Toby and he met again for the first time since the incident. They became, if not friends, acquaintances at least, and occasionally had a drink together in the college bar.)

8

RACIALISM

Dear Mrs Asquith

Of course you will find racial prejudice here just as you will find every other human weakness. But appearances can be deceptive. The cry of 'Come on, Nigger!' which jars so painfully upon your liberal susceptibilities, may have no racial significance either for the speaker or for the Nigerian boy. You assume that 'the Nigerian boy must be deeply offended even if he does not show it'. You may be right; he has lived in a school community long enough to know how to disguise his feelings. But I doubt whether he has to in this case. He is a popular boy, a good athlete and a mature personality. I think he accepts the word 'nigger' for what it is: a nickname inspired by affection not prejudice.

This may sound like a headmaster's special pleading. Explicit racialism is as common among the affluent young as it is on the football terraces. No point in denying that. I just do not believe that this is an example of it.

I will risk provoking you by adding that the use of this nickname may be positively helpful to racial tolerance. It gets the racial difference out in the open. I am all for controlling one's racial prejudice, but not suppressing it or pretending it does not exist. The English middle class can be as hypocritical about race as their Victorian forebears were about sex. Feelings of guilt force them to put on the respectability of tolerance. There is something honest about that cry of 'Come on, Nigger!'

You want me to speak to the boys and to make sure they never use that word again. I do not think that is a wise course. Such a ban is unenforceable and would look pretty odd when the boys must know that I have been aware of the nickname for some time. But much more important, the ban would activate a conflict that they have found a way of making relatively harmless. 'Nigger – oh, sorry, we're not allowed to call you that, are we?' they would say. 'You're a protected species, you know.' And no doubt much worse. There are times when it is best to leave what is not perfect alone.

This will not convince you that the school is 'doing all in its power to eliminate racial prejudice'. But then I do not believe that it can be eliminated. I think it can be controlled in oneself and contained in society: and that it should be towards those objectives that the school's policy should be directed.

Tolerance is a matter of self-control, isn't it? We are not born tolerant. Our instinct is for survival. The more confident we feel about that, the more we can lower our own guard. But fear of what is strange never leaves us entirely. We learn to control it, partly for our self-respect (we don't wish to think of ourselves as prejudiced) and partly because we crave public respect. If racial prejudice becomes respectable – as it does from time to time – we can let our control ease a little and we find that rather a relief.

I think of myself as a tolerant man but I know that the potential for prejudice is always there. I can have friendly dealings with a person of another race almost without being conscious of any difference. But if he should insult me or provoke me in some other way, then I am acutely conscious that he is of a different race. The prejudice pushes itself forward because it is a weapon I can use in my anger and frustration. I may not express it openly – the controls still operate that far at least – but inside my head the controls have loosened. The anger passes and the tolerance reasserts itself.

No one but myself knows how close I came to calling him a nigger.

I think that is a fair description of how most people experience their own racial prejudices. When you tell me that you honestly believe that you are incapable of such prejudice I am sceptical, as I am when a pacifist tells me he is incapable of violence. There are no unprejudiced people, only those who have their prejudices under control and those who do not. To pretend otherwise is to mislead the young. No doubt from time to time there are saintly figures whose self-control is such that it is no longer needed. But saints are bad models for children. They are in a different race. 'The speed of a runaway horse does not count,' said Jean Cocteau. Saints are runaway horses. What the young need is a model of maturity that is within their grasp. By all means let a headmaster hold out an ideal to his pupils but he must never pretend that anyone, least of all himself, is likely to achieve it.

What I am aiming at here is to put before the boys and girls a realistic, attainable goal – racial prejudice not eliminated but successfully controlled and contained. That does not mean that I have a structured programme. I am by nature an opportunist, a most useful quality in a headmaster. When the opportunity occurs – a homily in morning chapel, an informal discussion with senior pupils, the way I respond to a particular case – I argue for the pursuit of the realistic goal. Here, in rather rambling, anecdotal form, is how that opportunism works.

Anti-semitism is the oldest form of racial prejudice that schools have had to deal with. It is still around. Last year I saw a notice on a houseboard on which the words 'No Jews' had been written across the list of the house football team. I was tempted to lecture the school at assembly but I didn't. Nor do I think the Jewish pupils would have wished me to do so. I took the notice down. You tread a narrow path between wanting to be seen to condemn racialism and knowing that what the boys would regard as an over-reaction would lead them to dismiss your embarrassed liberalism as humbug.

However, there are times when a headmaster must take positive action. Last term a Jewish parent complained that his fourteen-year-old son had been subjected to racial harassment which on the face of it was intolerable. His history class was studying the Second World War. When they started to discuss the concentration camps, the other boys challenged the truth of the historical facts and the Jewish boy found himself trying to convince them that the holocaust had actually occurred. The master was inexperienced and allowed the argument to go on too long before he realized what was happening. The Jewish boy was the cleverest in a class of clever boys; he was top in almost every subject. The master had inadvertently provided the mob with an occasion to express their envy and resentment. The Jewish boy rose to the bait, not least because a number of his relations had been murdered in the camps.

Once they knew that he was sensitive on the issue, the other boys continued the baiting out of school. They used phrases such as: 'Weren't the gas chambers enough for you?' 'yid', 'kike', 'we have ways of turning you to ashes'. Not surprisingly his father insisted that I should take steps to put a stop of this 'moronic behaviour'.

I saw the boys concerned and told them, perhaps more angrily than I felt, that what they had been doing was a cruel form of bullying and 'totally unacceptable in a school like this'. How often that word 'unacceptable' comes to a headmaster's lips. How often he adds 'in a school like this' as though the boys' offences would hardly be noticed in the local comprehensive. The boys said they were sorry and that they had not meant any harm. They weren't and they had but now they knew that the next time the consequences would be more serious.

As far as I know the hounding of the Jewish boy stopped.

There were no more complaints. The mob had expressed their frustration at his maddening success and returned to more routine pastimes. Was it an example of racial prejudice? In one sense it must be counted as such. But that is not the whole truth. Five of the other boys in the class were Jewish. They joined in the baiting as vigorously as the rest, obeying the oldest law in the schoolboy jungle – hunt or be hunted. I doubt whether the cause of the baiting was racial prejudice. It was mediocrity's revenge on excellence. Racialism was the weapon to hand. And the language the baiters used should not be taken at its face value; the self-conscious callousness of the adolescent shocks adults rather than contemporaries. When the American spacecraft exploded, killing all seven astronauts, there were many sick jokes circulating in the Knightsbridge pubs frequented by the fashionable young. 'What does NASA stand for? Need Another Seven Astronauts!' Just as when Cambodiáns were dying in their hundreds of thousands from starvation the unwary parents were asked: 'What's the fastest thing on two legs? A Cambodian with a luncheon voucher.'

I saw the Jewish boy on his own. He was embarrassed, giving the impression that he could handle the situation, and resented his father's intervention and mine. I remembered reading about the Jewish writer, Hannah Arendt, who encountered anti-semitism at her school in East Prussia before the First World War. Her mother's instructions were explicit. If any of the teachers made anti-semitic remarks Hannah was to go home at once, leaving it to her mother to complain to the school authorities. But if the other children made anti-semitic remarks, Hannah was to deal with that in her own way and never mention it at home. The Jewish boy would have agreed with Hannah's mother.

Can schools teach pupils to be tolerant? I do not think there is any doubt that they should try but there is disagreement on how to do it. One approach is to let children learn tolerance from the example of adults; it is not taught in the classroom, it is learnt day by day, term by term, as the attitude of the staff and of the school as a community are revealed. The other approach is that you cannot leave it to chance and must ensure that all pupils receive teaching specifically designed to develop a tolerant attitude. The English tradition has on the whole favoured the former approach: right attitudes are caught not taught; in a good school they are in the air the pupils breathe. But that aristocratic and rather civilized view can easily be a cover for a headmaster's inertia or reluctance to tackle an awkward issue. At the other extreme, the determination to teach children to be tolerant by a course of instruction can have a negative effect. When Bernard Shaw said that 'education is everything you remember when you have forgotten everything you learnt at school', he was only emphasizing the obvious point that formal education is shed much more quickly than what we learn informally. How much do you remember of what you were taught in the classroom?

You will not be surprised to learn that where values such as tolerance, honesty, fortitude are concerned, I prefer the informal, opportunistic approach. I teach early modern history to the sixth form. There is no shortage of illustrations of man's inhumanity to man in that period and they have the advantage of being more remote than apartheid or Gulag or Belsen. The anger we feel when we read of the Massacre of St Bartholomew's Eve is not dictated by fashion. It has an honesty that is hard to achieve in our response to contemporary horrors.

The historical approach has other advantages. It can remind us, not too painfully, that there is nothing especially creditable about the record of our own country. The Elizabethans who crushed pregnant women to death for harbouring Jesuit priests would have found little difficulty fitting into Gestapo uniforms.

An even more valuable lesson of history is that the problem we are wrestling with is not religious bigotry or racial hatred;

they are merely the instruments through which the human capacity for cruelty finds expression. The world our children are growing up in tries to persuade them that it is in racialism, not in human nature, that evil has its origin; and that if we could eliminate racial prejudice all would be sweetness and light. In much the same way, the men and women of the eighteenth-century Enlightenment imagined that if only they could eliminate religious superstition and bigotry, the age of cruelty would be replaced by the age of reason. Lucky for them they did not see the twentieth century.

You see my point. If I hammer away at racial prejudice, I not only risk a characteristic schoolboy 'turn-off', I may do worse harm by persuading my pupils to confuse the symptom with the disease. And if there is one thing I want to do for them, it is to help them to discriminate between fashionable pre-occupations and permanent truth. Human nature – I fear this is beginning to sound like a sermon – is a very permanent truth.

I am a poor headmaster if I cannot surround my pupils with sufficient men and women whose clear thinking and self-control on this issue are catching. But attitudes to race may also be influenced by the school's policy on entry. Does it operate a Jewish quota? Does it keep a discreet watch on the number of Asian candidates in the entrance exam? It is not open to the maintained schools to control their entry in this way but most independent schools do.

The days of the official Jewish quota have gone, partly I think because independent schools have become more en-lightened, but also because they do not wish to be seen dis-criminating on the grounds of race. Some discrimination occurs all the same. The argument is that these schools are Christian foundations and cannot dilute the Christian content too far without changing the nature of the school and betray-ing the wishes of the founders. It would be just as naive to believe that this is the school's only motive as it would be to assume that the Christian foundation argument is complete hypocrisy. It is not as simple as that. The Christian foundation argument is not disreputable though in a secular society it has an increasingly hollow ring. What has cast doubt on the sincerity of headmasters who use this argument is their willingness to open their doors to children of other faiths when they are short of applicants. Where Jewish children have found it difficult to gain admission, Moslems and Hindus are welcomed, if not with open arms, at least with relief that they can pay the fees.

If a policy on Jewish applicants does exist then it is better that it operates in the open. One school uses the following formula:

> I am afraid we are unable to accept his name onto our lists. The reason is that the school has a close affiliation with the Church of England and it is therefore not possible for us to accept more than a small proportion of non-Christian pupils. I hope you will believe, even though you may not agree with this policy, that in pursuing it we are not acting from motives of religious prejudice. We have always had some Jewish pupils in the school and have no intention whatsoever of ceasing to do so.

That is honestly stated and I see no reason why we should jump to the conclusion that it is a cloak for anti-semitism. That anti-semitism can exist I have no doubt but I do not believe it is common. One of the worst examples I have come across is in the interview notes made by the man in charge of entry at an independent school in the Sixties. Of one parent he wrote: 'The father was fat, Jewish and unattractive,' and of a couple who wished to register their son, 'Both parents came to the interview. Very Hebraic. I formed the impression that they did not like soap and water.'

We have never as far as I know operated a Jewish quota but when I arrived I found that Jews were barred from scholarships, which were exclusively for boys who were 'British born and members of the Church of England'. I removed these qualifications, which had no historical justification – they had been introduced in the Fifties – and which excluded good candidates. How far I was motivated by a dislike of religious and racial discrimination, I am not sure. A headmaster's motives for reform are almost always complex and are just as likely to include a desire to make his mark as a determination to follow his convictions. Nor can I be sure that my action inspired greater tolerance among the pupils. It certainly encouraged more Jewish boys to apply, and not just as scholars: the percentage of Jewish pupils has more than doubled in my time here. That does not eliminate anti-semitism but it signals to the school and to the world at large that we are opposed to that form of discrimination.

Before you think too well of me, I must tell you that soon after I had opened the scholarships to non-Christians and foreigners, I began to be concerned at the number of Asian and Arab boys coming forward to take the entrance exam. If the number had increased I think I should have tried to control it. In other words I should have been prepared to introduce some form of quota.

My attitudes are not so contradictory as you might suppose. I opened the scholarships to all-comers because the school's interests and my own opposition to discrimination coincided. In the case of the Asian and Arab boys there was no such coincidence; a high proportion of Asian and Arab boys might have deterred other parents. A headmaster is not paid to make the world a better place; he is paid to keep the school full.

I wonder what Nigger would say if he could read all this? When we spoke about racial prejudice one evening last term, he was down to earth. Yes, it occurred, particularly among young boys. Yes, it had worried him in his first year but he had learnt to handle it. In the sixth form it was rare. When I asked him if he thought the school ought to be doing more to discourage racial prejudice, he said something along these

86

lines: 'No. It's going to happen anyway. You can't stop it altogether. If teachers try, they often make it worse because they get it out of perspective. One piece of racial aggro and some teachers will devote a whole lesson to what happened in the concentration camps. If it is organized or if some young kids are being bullied, masters ought to do something about it. But nine times out of ten it isn't really racialism, it's just frustration – Monday morning, lousy lunch, double physics, whatever makes people irritable. In which case it's best', and here he seemed to be imitating my voice, 'to treat it with the contempt it deserves.'

I think his advice and that of Hannah Arendt's mother are what I would pass on to you as a parent. If there is a clear case of racial prejudice it should be scotched. But what boys, particularly young boys, say to one another is seldom worth losing any sleep over.

Yours sincerely

JOHN RAE

9

SMOKING, DRINKING
AND DRUGS

Dear Mr and Mrs Paisley

I'm afraid I cannot give you a precise answer. On the use of drugs, particularly illegal ones, there is a conspiracy of silence in independent schools. No one knows how widespread the problem is. But I will explain to you my policy. If you are thinking of sending Jonathan here you have a right to know.

Cigarette smoking is as widespread as it ever was among teenagers in all types of school. Which raises the interesting question of why the anti-smoking campaign, which has had a significant impact on adults, has failed so lamentably to deter the young.

I am astonished at the naivety of the material that is aimed at young people of eleven to fourteen. But there is a more fundamental reason why adolescents ignore the warnings: they cannot focus on the reality of death. If adults say that smoking can kill, but not for fifty years, the warning has no meaning. At the same time, some adolescents enjoy the idea of dicing with death. They deliberately bring death into sharp focus in an attempt to understand it but this also serves to make the distant hazards of smoking look irrelevant. A young man who is prepared to drive a motorcycle at 100 mph for kicks is unlikely to be frightened when you tell him that smoking may damage his health. One way or another, the adolescent is programmed to be immune to the medical evidence.

That may explain why the young are not deterred. But what leads them to want to smoke in the first place? There are several different but overlapping answers.

Cigarette advertising is much more sophisticated than the counter-blast and much of it is directed at the young. The manufacturers know what the young do not, that those who start smoking in adolescence are the most likely to be hooked for life. Which is why I am in favour of bribing children not to smoke before they are twenty-one. Psychologists and moralists may disapprove but I am all for preventing smoking by appealing to greed. If you are thinking of making an offer to Jonathan, the going rate is between £500 and £1000 among the affluent boys here and one boy has been offered a Porsche if he can reach twenty-one without smoking.

More powerful than the advertiser's guile is the peer group pressure. It starts early and is at its most intense at about the age of fourteen. It happens at parties, on the bus home, or during school expeditions, and it can be hard to resist. Smoking is still seen by adolescents as a grown-up activity. Above all, it is a weapon against the two great enemies – anxiety and boredom. It is no accident that smoking became a popular habit in the First World War when extremes of boredom and anxiety characterized life in the trenches. For the insecure adolescent, smoking is a way of acquiring self-confidence, of projecting a cool image and of covering shyness. I gave cigarettes up in my thirties but I can remember what a comfort it was when arriving at a party where I knew no one, to have that reassuring routine: tapping your jacket pocket, feeling the firm shape of the packet, jacking up a cigarette with a flick of your wrist, placing it in the corner of your mouth, lighting it and drawing in one deep breath while slightly narrowing your eyes like Humphrey Bogart in *Casablanca*.

Despite the pressures from their contemporaries, adolescents are still susceptible to the influence of adults. Parents who smoke more often than not have children who smoke. Schools that take a permissive line will have many more smokers than schools that are prepared to enforce a ban. There is no need to place smoking in the category of major crime but my experience has been that treating smoking as a disciplinary question is more likely to deter boys and girls than regarding it solely as a question of health education. The latter is important but ineffective on its own. Together, information and discipline at least have a chance of reducing smoking in the school precincts. Outside the school gate the adolescent smoker hastens to the shadows for a quick drag before going home. 'Got a light, guv?' one of our fourteen-year-olds asked the man behind him in the bus queue. The man was indeed a governor – of the school. That is just the sort of bad luck young smokers need.

The battle against smoking is a never-ending one that we will not win, a guerrilla war in which our sense of having the situation under control is an illusion. But we cannot give up because if we fail to make a stand against smoking, the adolescent will move that much more easily into experimentation with illegal drugs.

Alcohol presents a different problem. Drinking is socially acceptable and I have never regarded it as my job to encourage boys to become teetotallers. I am to stop them drinking illegally or excessively. The school rules ban those under eighteen from pubs and make it an offence for any pupil to bring alcohol into the school. We are more effective at enforcing the latter than the former. Boys do not find it difficult to slip out to the pub and they are unlikely to be caught unless they drink too much. That is not a bad arrangement. Unlike smoking or the use of illegal drugs, teenage drinking does not carry with it the risks of becoming hooked. Adult alcoholism has its roots in adult problems not in the excesses of youth.

Young people have to learn to manage alcohol. The school rule is intended to operate like a speed limit in a built-up area. If you are caught breaking the rule, you are punished (and if you go on breaking it you will be suspended). The rule does not prevent all drinking any more than a speed limit prevents all speeding; but it deters some and slows down others. The pupils learn moderation because it is in their interests to do so. The young are going to drink anyway; trying to stop them altogether is neither justified by the chances of success nor required by the nature of the crime. If they leave here able to recognize and draw back from that moment when one more swig will push them over the edge, I reckon I shall have done a good job.

There is no way I could adopt that attitude to the use of illegal drugs. There is an element of lottery, of Russian roulette, about using even cannabis. These drugs are *not* in the same category as alcohol and tobacco.

When I became a headmaster in the late Sixties, the first fears about drug abuse were experienced in independent schools. Within twenty years it has become one of the principal worries for parents, though many of the schools still act as though their pupils were not at risk. Headmasters and head-mistresses who assure parents that there is no drug problem in their school deceive themselves as well as the parents. There may be no drugs at that moment on the campus, but I would swear that in every secondary school in the country there are boys and girls who have experimented with cannabis at least and who are at risk of becoming more seriously involved. Just because the experimentation takes place away from the school does not mean that it is not the school's problem. Not only do those pupils who use drugs in the holidays or at home need help; sooner or later they will bring drugs into the school and involve others.

The heads of independent schools are very reluctant to talk about drugs, even – or especially – to each other. It is the old problem of competition. A conference of restaurateurs is hardly likely to have 'Cockroaches in the Kitchen' on its agenda. While the heads' reluctance is understandable, their eagerness to drop broad hints to parents that the problem of drugs *will* be found in other schools suggests that these academic gentlemen are in no position to look down on the morals of the marketplace.

Heads have three responsibilities in relation to illegal drugs. First, to have an unequivocal rule banning the possession or use of drugs. Secondly, to ensure that parents and teaching staff are sufficiently well informed to deal with the subject when it is raised by the pupils, as it certainly will be. Thirdly, to provide a programme of health education that leaves the pupils in no doubt about the dangers of drug abuse.

When I first became a headmaster I made the mistake of thinking that the rules could distinguish between pupils who experimented, who could be forgiven, and those who dealt in drugs, who should be expelled. In practice the distinction is far from clear. There are pupils in every school at one time or another who provide (rather than push) drugs. But to expel the provider while allowing his customers to remain only confuses the pupils as to the school's attitude. Is the school opposed to the use of drugs or not? I am convinced that my ambivalent policy led some boys into regular drug abuse. The unambiguous rule that I introduced some years later (whereby any use of drugs inside or outside the school leads to automatic expulsion) did not eliminate drug abuse but by raising the stakes it did make pupils think twice before taking the risk.

Heads who do not expel pupils who are known to have used drugs argue that the more flexible approach keeps open the channel of communication and enables the school to help those who are at risk of becoming involved. That is wishful thinking. Any ambivalence on the school's part will be interpreted by the pupils as a green light to have a go.

The hard line has to be underpinned by a well-informed

body of parents and staff. Many parents and teachers are not only ignorant but positively resist being educated in the facts of drug abuse. One of the major problems for heads is that some members of staff are equivocal about the seriousness of the drug problem and others just don't want to know. I have no patience with either. Teachers cannot be equivocal about breaking the law nor can they close their eyes to contemporary life by posing as amiable but other-worldly scholars. Inside the absent-minded professor lurks a moral coward.

Some parents are similarly equivocal or escapist. And some use illegal drugs themselves. But the majority want to know the facts about the drugs their children might come into contact with: what do the drugs look like? Where can they be bought and at what price? What are the tell-tale signs of drug using? What action should they take if they suspect their son or daughter is using drugs? They do not want to hear an intellectual argument about the role of drugs in different human societies. They regard the problem as more urgent and they resent the detached, philosophical approach adopted by some speakers. I have found that doctors and psychiatrists in particular are unwilling to condemn the use of illegal drugs. They will explain why they think people take drugs and what the medical and psychological consequences are, but they are reluctant to say that drug taking is wrong. They shun moral judgement as though it were a form of superstition that would cast doubt on their status as scientists.

What arguments can parents use? When I talk to all the thirteen-year-old new boys on the subject I give them the factual information and I explain why I moved from a flexible rule to automatic expulsion. I do not exaggerate the dangers of smoking cannabis or claim that its use will inevitably lead on to the use of harder drugs. I use the Russian roulette argument.

In the last ten years two former pupils of mine have died from the abuse of drugs. They started to use cannabis while still at school. Popular opinion expressed by adults as well as by their contemporaries was that cannabis was no more harmful than nicotine or alcohol. What they were not told was that *some* personalities are inexorably drawn from soft drugs to hard. Such people are in a minority but so is the single round in the revolver chamber. The trouble with using soft drugs is that you do not know before you start whether you are a member of this minority. There *is* a risk therefore that smoking cannabis will lead an individual on to heroin and, in some cases, to death. That risk is not present in the use of nicotine and alcohol and it should make parents vigilant. Drugs, with the exception of cocaine, are not expensive but they still present cashflow problems to most users. Parents who find money disappearing at home may well have a son who is pushed to pay for his drugs.

Parents can take other precautions. Boys and girls are first offered drugs by their 'friends', particularly at parties. It is not easy for parents to monitor their children's friends but if they are suspicious they should contact the school. Though the school may not have hard evidence, it is usually in a position to say whether the 'friend' is a possible drug risk. Detaching your son or daughter from a 'risky friend' is even harder: it almost always causes resentment and at first is likely to be ignored. But it is better to express your fears than remain silent. Just because your advice is spurned does not mean that it will have no effect. It is a warning that your son or daughter may find useful at a critical time.

Checking on the parties to which your children have been invited can also provoke an angry response. But it is well worth doing. Telephone the host's parents. Are they going to be present? How many people have been invited? If nothing else, it shows that you care. Hardly a term goes by without it being reported to me that parents have gone away for the weekend leaving their teenage son or daughter to organize a party in their house. The parents are shocked when they return and discover that the party got out of hand, with gatecrashers bringing their cannabis and pills with them, the drinks cupboard raided and cigarette ends stubbed out on the carpet. The parents' first reaction is to blame the school. 'If we had known that this is how your boys behave, Headmaster, we would never have sent our son to your school.' To which I am tempted to reply, 'If I had known how selfish and irresponsible his parents were, I would never have accepted him.'

What makes me angry in such cases is my belief that it is the accidental encounter with drugs that is the principal reason why young people start taking them. When a boy or girl becomes a habitual user, we should look for an explanation in their personality, but the first step is so often just a matter of being with the wrong friends at the wrong place at the wrong time. One of the first duties of schools and parents, therefore, is to restrict the opportunities. A hard disciplinary line on drug abuse may only serve to drive the problem away from the school campus, but by doing so it restricts the opportunities of being offered drugs. I would never send my son or daughter to a school which allowed a drug user to remain; I have witnessed too much degradation and tragedy that has been caused by what was thought to be a 'flexible and tolerant' policy.

Some adolescents will find an opportunity whatever precautions are taken. Increasingly, the opportunity is to use heroin and cocaine rather than cannabis. Cheap, high purity heroin is plentiful. The switch to sniffing from injecting has made its use widespread. If it has not yet hit the independent schools, it soon will. Cocaine, too, is more widely available and is used by the fashionable young of both sexes. What is it that makes them seize the opportunity when it comes? Sometimes they experiment because they wish to be thought daring or because they enjoy the corrupt or sinister reputation that an aura of drugginess confers upon them. When I was sixteen, I cultivated a reputation for wild and self-destructive behaviour; the idea of the talented youth going to the devil, of the poet dying young, strongly appealed to me, as did the anxiety and concern my antics provoked in my contemporaries. It isn't fame that is the spur at that age so much as the need to assert your separate identity. I attract attention, therefore I am.

In the Forties you could do the Boys Own Byron bit and still grow up unharmed. Drugs have changed all that. They have brought the adult world of serious consequences into the innocent escapades of youth. It was once possible to take a detached view of adolescent behaviour because you knew it would pass. You cannot shrug your shoulders at drugs and say, 'They'll grow out of it.' Some will, but others, on the contrary, will grow more deeply into it until they become dependent or addicted. I cannot think of any problem faced by the young of previous generations that so insidiously appealed to the weakness of human nature. The generations who grew up in war-time or in poverty seem fortunate by comparison. Drug abuse is not just a modern version of the age-old problem of growing up. It has changed the nature of the problem. The solution does not lie in the pursuit and punishment of criminals or in effective health education, important though they are. The only sure defence against drug abuse lies in the willpower of the individual.

It cannot be said too often (but is hardly said at all) that involvement in drug abuse is a sign of weakness of character. Strange how that phrase jars on some people as though weakness of character, like racial superiority, was no longer an acceptable concept. But I do not think it helps the young if we confuse the reason for being tempted with the reason for giving in. Unhappiness, bravado, despair, frustration may all provide the occasion for temptation but it is lack of willpower, lack of strength of character, that is the cause of surrender.

I emphasize this because too many adults talk about the drug problem as though it is a sort of Black Death against which the individual has no defence. They use the terminology of disease; drug abuse is said to have reached 'epidemic proportions'. By denying the element of personal choice, they encourage a sense of inevitability.

There is nothing inevitable about drug abuse. No one *has* to take illegal drugs; the compulsion is in their own minds. This is something I try to drive home to the young boys here. True freedom is freedom from those compulsions that eliminate our ability to choose. The father who *must* have a drink when he returns from the office; the mother who *must* take a sleeping pill; the son or daughter who *must* have a cigarette, are slaves to their compulsions like the child who *must* look under the bed before turning out the light. The boys understand the grip of such compulsions because they have experienced them as children; a vital step towards freedom for every child is the night when he wills himself not to look under the bed even though he knows that the assassins and monsters are packed tight there like sardines. In the morning he leaps out of bed a free man.

I put before these boys an ideal of maturity free from all compulsions. A mature man is not compelled to do anything. He is utterly free and in control of his own life. I don't mean that he has suppressed his emotions; suppression is the technique used by the weak-willed who dare not risk losing control. The strong-willed man does not suppress his emotions; he lives at peace with them because he knows that he can manage them.

Does that sound as if I am idealizing some Nietzschean superman? I assure you, I am not. The ideal of the mature man, who can steer his life through the cross-currents of fears and desires, underlies almost all our ideas about the upbringing of children. Even if we don't articulate it, as parents we understand instinctively that we must teach our children self-discipline. The strength of character to say 'no' is crucial to their survival. And it is the only certain defence against the threat of drug abuse. The young men and women who become degenerate, requiring stronger and stronger and more and more frequent stimulants, until they destroy themselves, have not been killed by the Mafia as is popularly supposed; they have killed themselves with the help of their parents, who failed to instil in them the discipline of self-denial.

I hope this makes clear my attitude to smoking, drinking and drugs. If you do not like it, then you should not send Jonathan here. If you are in broad agreement with my approach, we can work together to help him face these problems.

Yours sincerely

JOHN RAE

10

CORPORAL PUNISHMENT

Dear Mr Moriarty

So much has been written about corporal punishment that I hesitate to answer your letter. But since I have no intention of reintroducing the practice, you have a right to know why. You are correct in saying that some independent schools still use the cane and that there is nothing in law to prevent me using it here.

I was beaten at school and, when I became a prefect, I beat other boys. In my first headmastership I used the cane. When I came here I found that corporal punishment had recently fallen into disuse; there had been no formal act of abolition. There is no way, while I am headmaster, that it will be revived.

My experience leads me to the following conclusions: First, that corporal punishment contributes nothing to good discipline in a school, though it may help to contain the more extreme forms of disruptive behaviour. Secondly, that the psychological effects are an important consideration, though the emphasis is too often placed on the effect on the boy and not enough on the motivation of the master.

The distinction I place on the difference between promoting good discipline and containing bad is not just a debating point. There are times in the history of institutions when good discipline is not a realistic goal. When armies were recruited from the criminal riff-raff of society, flogging was needed to limit the damage done by disobedience and desertion. But in a modern army such as ours, the quality of the recruits as well as their commitment to the enterprise mean that commanders can think in terms of encouraging good discipline and in this context flogging has no place.

A similar though not exactly parallel development occurred in schools. In medieval and early modern schools, the long and dull curriculum meant that the birch was the only way to keep the boys awake. In sixteenth-century Cambridge, a new graduate destined for schoolmastering demonstrated his prowess by ceremonially flogging a volunteer, called a 'shrewd boy', who received four pence for his trouble. The rod was so much the dominant feature of school life that men noted that they dreamt of school whippings twenty years afterwards. In the late eighteenth and early nineteenth centuries, the old public schools were often in a state of near anarchy and headmasters had to flog their way out of trouble.

That flogging remained the norm after order had been restored was a reflection not so much of its effectiveness as of the national belief that this was still the best way to bring the old Adam to heal. Judicial flogging in this country was only abolished in 1948, its departure being hastened when two ex-public schoolboys were given the cat-o'-nine-tails for their part in robbery with violence. But corporal punishment continued in schools long after it had disappeared from the rest of society and long after it had been abolished as a suitable punishment for children in other European countries. The British found it difficult to dissociate the idea of school discipline from the use of corporal punishment; they just could not believe that the rougher elements could be contained without the threat of the cane. It was a habit of mind rather than a rational assessment. Progressive schools might talk about putting the emphasis on promoting good discipline but the tradition put the emphasis firmly on containing the bad.

The present situation illustrates my point. By 1986, most independent schools had abandoned corporal punishment. It did not mean that the pupils had become angels; there had been a gradual shift away from containing bad discipline to promoting good. The key to that change was, as you would expect, an improvement in the relations between masters and boys. The arrival of girls in the sixth form accelerated the change. It is no accident that the few independent schools that still use the cane are ones that have remained exclusively single-sex.

People have been claiming for the last hundred years that relations between masters and boys have been improving so I must not exaggerate. What happened, particularly in the much maligned Sixties, was that the gap between pupils and teachers narrowed to a point at which those in authority, whether masters or senior boys, found it increasingly difficult to contemplate the use of corporal punishment. It is often said that the disappearance of the cane has improved relations within a school. No doubt this is true but I think that what really happened was that improved relations undermined the basis on which the cane was used. When the hierarchy which set boys and masters in a fixed relationship broke down, corporal punishment was bound to go. In practice this meant that the authorities in independent schools were now more inclined to tackle the causes of anti-social behaviour than merely to punish its manifestations. When I was at school, a boy who was disruptive in class would have been beaten. Today he will still be punished but in the context of his house-master making some attempt to discover why he is behaving in that way. It is more time-consuming but in the end more effective.

Once you have accepted the idea that punishment is not enough, it is very difficult to justify the use of the cane. You cannot expect a housemaster to discuss with a boy the reasons for his disruptive behaviour and then say, 'Right, now that we have got that straight, I am going to beat you.'

A headmaster who demands the right to retain corporal

punishment may, from his point of view, be correct if he judges that the discipline is so bad that only corporal punishment can contain it. The behaviour of some of the pupils in inner city state schools resembles that of the public schoolboys in the eighteenth century. I am not sure that if I were their headmaster I would be prepared to abandon corporal punishment. The abolitionists will regard my pragmatic approach as a cop-out. 'Are you *for* corporal punishment or *against*?' I am against it but I would not deny to a colleague working with much more difficult children than I have ever had to face, the right to decide for himself whether to use it or not.

In a school like this there would have to be an extraordinary breakdown of 'law and order' to justify the reintroduction of the cane. The head of a modern independent school has a great deal going for him when it comes to keeping discipline: he can expel, he can call on the active co-operation of the parents and he knows that on this matter most pupils are prepared to come to an accommodation with the school authorities. If the head of an independent school cannot keep good discipline, he had better seek another line of employment.

In these circumstances, corporal punishment is wrong because it is unnecessary. The old boys of the school sometimes regret – or perhaps resent – the passing of the cane. 'It never did us any harm,' is a drearily familiar assertion in the club bar. I wonder. The historical evidence for a causal connection between corporal punishment and a taste for flagellation is, at first sight, convincing. I gather from your letter that you are sceptical about the psychological damage done by corporal punishment. You are wise to be so, given some of the oversimplified connections that are made, but the historical evidence is worth considering.

Flagellation is often referred to as the English vice. It still flourishes, to judge by the nature of much of our pornography and by the services offered by the oldest profession. For over three hundred years it has been taken for granted that the Englishman's desire to be whipped has its origin in the use of corporal punishment in schools. In Thomas Shadwell's Restoration farce *The Virtuoso*, first produced in 1676, one of the male characters, Snare, asks his mistress to flog him. 'I wonder,' she comments, 'that should please you so much that pleases me so little.' To which Snare replies, 'I was so used to it at Westminster School, I could never leave off it since.' Swinburne, who was mercilessly beaten at Eton, could never leave off it either, though in his case the addiction was to fantasy, expressed in poetry and plays. But Swinburne's case, particularly his obsession with dominating female characters, suggests that the origin of his addiction was in his own temperament, which Eton's birches only confirmed. When he writes, 'One of the great charms of birching lies in the sentiment that the floggee is the powerless victim of the furious rage of a beautiful woman,' one is bound to ask whether corporal punishment had anything to do with it. If the masochistic tendency had its origin in a particular experience, is it not more likely that this was in the nursery and in infancy?

Swinburne's public school contemporaries were no less addicted to flagellation but they pursued their not so off-beat entertainment with a gusto that seems healthy compared with Swinburne's fantasies. Such was the demand for flagellation it required a variety of professionals and amateurs to satisfy it. The professionals were ladies, such as the famous Mrs Collet of Covent Garden, whose confidential establishments catered to the taste for flagellation. The amateurs organized parties and dining clubs for enthusiasts. Dinner at the Block Club was followed by flogging for the members, while those lucky (or unlucky) enough to be invited to Lord Abingdon's parties found that the guests were expected to participate in public flagellation, either as victims or holders down. Men who preferred to suffer in private kept a cane handy in their wives' or mistresses' bedrooms. The Victorian upper classes were a very kinky lot but their antics strike a hilarious rather than a pathological note. Are we correct in thinking of these men as psychologically damaged? I doubt it. Unlike Swinburne, they appear to have led normal sex lives despite or perhaps because of their excursions to Mrs Collet's and their nights out at the Block Club. So I am sceptical of the claim that corporal punishment in schools produces aberrant psychosexual tendencies in the form of masochism. I suspect the worst it can do is to make a young man aware of an aspect of his personality that is either innate or owes its development to experience long before schooldays.

Victorian kinkiness could take a less hilarious form. For the many who acquired a taste for being beaten, there were undoubtedly a few whose power to beat both awakened and satisfied their desire to cause pain. The sadistic master is a familiar character in the boyhood of those of us who were sent to boarding school. When I was ten or thereabouts, I fell foul of a master of whom I can remember little except that he was determined to beat me. I had done a piece of work with which he was not satisfied. He ordered me to do it again properly or be beaten. I did it not once but three times and each time I took it to him in his room he found some trivial fault with it. The last time he tore it up in a very precise, deliberate manner and sent me out to the playing fields to cut a switch for my own execution. No one could persuade me that he was not sadistic. Did the headmaster have no inkling that the man was not fit to be put in authority over boys? Almost certainly not. There was no one to tell him. I never mentioned the incident to my parents, indeed I cannot remember mentioning it to anyone until now, and that is forty-five years too late.

That such men have always been drawn towards the teaching profession is evident from the history of our public schools. Even in the seventeenth century, when flogging was commonplace in society, it was condemned in schools because it 'fed the depraved sexual appetites of perverted pedagogues'. In an anonymous Victorian attack on beating, the author complains that too often the pretext for the punishment was not the offence of the boy but 'an unquenchable fire in the appetite of the master'. A cane in the hands of a senior boy or prefect presents the same temptation, as anyone who has held that power will know.

This is surely the real danger of corporal punishment, that it should be in the hands of anyone who has an appetite for using it. By restricting the power to the headmaster alone, you reduce that danger but do not eliminate it altogether. The danger of abuse is always there.

It is true that as a headmaster I sometimes feel that for a particular offence, six of the best would be less disruptive of a boy's education than sending him home, but if I reintroduced corporal punishment it would be an admission of failure.

One final point. You imply in your letter that the outcry against corporal punishment is symptomatic of 'the permissiveness that has taken hold of this country in recent years'. That is not the case. The outcry was as loud if not louder two hundred years ago. It has nothing to do with 'permissiveness'. In 1792 Robert Southey, the future poet laureate, was expelled from this school for writing a vehement protest against the excessive use of corporal punishment by the headmaster, Dr Vincent. Southey was one of those boys headmasters publicly praise but privately regret. He had a mind of his own and the courage to say what he thought. Appalled by the headmaster's predilection for flogging, he started a new school magazine called the *Flagellant*. The fifth issue carried his attack, though the article was unsigned. Corporal punishment was described as 'so beastly, so idolatrous a custom' that 'whosoever floggeth, that is, performeth the will of Satan, committeth an abomination'. Dr Vincent was furious. He bullied the publisher into revealing the name of the author and them promptly expelled

Southey. Southey was at first incredulous and then bitter. He wrote to a friend, 'I live in the charitable hope of one day dosing Vincent till I kill him.'

Dr Vincent survived. His method of imposing discipline did not. Southey's attack did not do the trick any more than the so-called permissiveness of our time. Corporal punishment has disappeared for the simple reason that enough people didn't want it any more. I doubt whether they looked upon it as a matter of principle; corporal punishment was an idea whose time had gone. You want to see it return. What you ask is not impossible but neither does it make sense. Even if I were convinced of the value of corporal punishment, I would no more reintroduce it than top hats and rolled umbrellas. That is not because I am permissive. It's just that I know a dead duck when I see one.

Yours sincerely

JOHN RAE

11

PARENTS SEPARATING

Dear David and Diana

Thank you for your letter telling me that you have decided to separate. You had warned me that this might happen but I am sad all the same to receive the news. We will do all we can to help Marcus find his way through what is bound to be at times a dark period of his life.

I have known you both for too long to mince my words. If I am blunt it is the bluntness of a friend, not of a headmaster pretending to be a marriage counsellor or playing God.

As far as Marcus is concerned your timing could hardly be worse. I think fourteen is the most vulnerable age. It is difficult enough at that age to know where you belong in the world without your parents adding to the uncertainty. And by coming to your decision in the middle of term you have made it more difficult to find the right moment – and for that matter the right place – to tell him.

You ask whether it might be better for me to tell him. I would if there was no other way. Some people think it is better for bad tidings to be borne by a stranger or at least by someone who is not emotionally involved. The theory is that the neutral figure helps to keep the emotional temperature low. The receiver of bad tidings cannot break down, certainly not if he is sitting forward on the sofa in the headmaster's study.

I am not sure that I believe in that approach. I know that we all have to learn how to take bad news. That is one thing none of us can escape. But surely it is better to be told by someone in whose love you feel secure, especially when you are young and vulnerable. It would be so much better if you told Marcus, both of you together and as soon as possible. He may suspect already. Don't leave it to someone else to confirm that suspicion. Which brings us to the practical problems of when and where.

Half term is two weeks away and Marcus will be coming home for a long weekend. You must tell him then. It isn't ideal: he will be coming back to school on Monday evening knowing that home as he has known it since his earliest memories of childhood will never be the same again. On the other hand it may well help him to be plunged back straight away into the rough and tumble of school life. Boarding schools do have their uses! So, the half term break is the time. You can't put it off till the end of term and you can't come down this weekend and tell him in the corner of a hotel lounge. Only last year some parents who were separating insisted on telling their son in the car parked outside the main school building. It was the end of Saturday morning and the drive was busy with other parents' cars and boys milling about. I could see the car clearly from the window. The boy was sitting in the back seat and the parents in the front. Mother had turned round but father was gripping the steering wheel as though he was anxious to get going. For most of the time, the boy had his face turned away from his parents and was staring blankly at the other boys hurrying away for the weekend.

I am not trying to tear-jerk you with vignettes of some English version of *Kramer Versus Kramer*. I just want to say that there is no ideal way of conveying the bad news but that some ways are worse than others.

When you do tell him, please don't lie. Don't tell him that you are going to live apart for an experimental period unless that is exactly what you intend. Don't give him false hopes.

He will want to know what is going to happen but I do not think he wants to be involved in a discussion of who goes where. As I understand it, home is going to be in Fulham with David, at least while Diana is on tour with the new play. Then what? Forgive me, Diana, if it sounds like male neo-colonialism, but I think home is where mother is. When our marriage was rocky, I tried looking after the children, and whatever else it was, it wasn't home. It isn't just that father is not there for enough of the time. Nor is it that – by nature or design? – he is domestically incompetent. It's something in the blood or the genes or the conditioning of God knows how long. Even under deep hypnosis, David can't be repro-grammed to create a home.

Marcus will ask, 'Where do I go for the holidays?' It's probably the only question he will ask. That reminds me of another lie to avoid. Don't try to sell him the idea of separation on the grounds that he will be better off: 'It'll be fun, really. You'll have two homes instead of one.' I need hardly tell you, he isn't stupid.

You will want to avoid melodrama but don't understate it too much. Phrases such as 'these things happen' and 'it's just one of those things' will hurt him because to him it is not just one of those things. Tell him straight. If you are both going to live with someone else, say so. Oddly enough, I think it may be easier for a boy to imagine his parents sleeping with some-one else than with each other. I know, he comes into your bed in the morning and all that, or at least he used to. But the mental image of his parents making love is something I suspect he shuts out. I may be generalizing from my own memories of being fourteen but I think it is a common experience. Any-way, if you are going to live with someone else, tell him that is what you are going to do. I think he can accept it more easily than you realize. What he does not want is to arrive home in the holidays to find a new 'uncle' or 'aunt' at the breakfast table.

I don't know how Marcus will react to the news of your separation. Tell him early in the weekend so that there is time for him to shut his mind to it for a while and still talk about it if he wants to before returning to school. When you do tell him, don't expect him to get worked up about it. He may shrug his shoulders. He may appear to take it in his stride. Or he may get up and slam the door in your face. He hasn't had a chance to think out how he wants to respond so I wouldn't put any interpretation on his reaction if I were you. And don't ask him what he thinks about it. He doesn't know.

I'm sorry, this is a list of don'ts and I have one more. Don't persuade yourself that he isn't going to be hurt. However careful you are, however amicable your agreement to go your separate ways, the only world he has ever known is falling apart. It is extraordinary how many parents think that they are so sensible and civilized about the end of their marriage that no damage will be done to those most dependent on its survival. A civilized separation is better than a bitter wrangle but the damage to the children cannot be avoided.

I would agree that a broken marriage is easier for the children to cope with than a breaking one. The tensions of a breaking marriage touch every corner of the home, so that every word or silence, every door opening or closing seems to threaten the brittle peace. The children watch and listen for the shooting war to start again. They know they may be used as decoys to draw the enemy's fire or as messengers required to traverse the no man's land between their parents' warring camps. When the tension is too great, they try their hand as peacemakers, a dangerous role when you are dealing with two people who will go to almost any lengths to avoid defeat.

The tensions are soon noticeable at school. More often than not the school will see the effects of a breaking marriage before the parents say anything about it. The boy's work and behaviour deteriorate. Even so, the school must sometimes seem to him a haven of calm, a rest camp away from the fighting. If he is a day boy he has to return to the front line every evening. At least the boarder is spared that. The other boys are not unsympathetic. They have either experienced the tension themselves or are well aware they might have to one day. They don't talk about it much with each other. There is no stigma attached to being the child of separated or divorced parents as there was when I was young (something akin to being illegitimate) though it is still something that boys are defensive about. But not sentimental: separating parents are too common. Most independent schools would put the proportion of pupils from single-parent families at between 20 and 30 per cent. The private day school at which I was teaching in New York had a figure of 50 per cent. When the casualties are that high, there is no place for sentiment. 'The bells of hell go ting-a-ling-a-ling for you but not for me.'

It is an unusual case for the break-up of a marriage to provoke conflict between boys. I recall one such case where the father of one boy went off with the mother of another. The boys, who had been friends, never spoke to one another afterwards, though whether that was hostility or embarrassment or loyalty to the parent left behind, I don't know.

If your separation has been preceded by a period of tension, it has not been reflected in Marcus's work or behaviour. I am glad of that. On the other hand, if he has had no forewarning, the news may be all the more disorientating. 'Like a chasm in a smooth road . . .', as Virginia Woolf wrote about the outbreak of the First World War. And now it comes back to me that last year when we were talking about Marcus you said that you made a point of not disagreeing with each other in front of him. So he may have no inkling that anything is wrong.

I have often thought that one of the disadvantages of boarding school is that the children may only see their parents' relationship at its best. You will laugh perhaps but I never once heard my parents quarrel. Maybe they never did. But I suspect they were on their best behaviour when we were home for the school holidays. The result was that when I got married, the first quarrels were shattering. I really thought we should have to be divorced! Children need to hear their parents quarrelling, don't they? It is an inescapable part of a relationship based on sexual attraction.

From the children's point of view there is the world of difference between a quarrel that can be healed in bed and the sort of guerrilla warfare that precedes the end of a marriage. And we must suppose that children can spot the difference. What worries me about Marcus is that there may have been no clues for him to spot. I saw him yesterday in Yard, kicking a ball about with his friends. It could have been just that it was the first really warm day after all that ice and snow, but he looked on top of the world. So be careful *how* you break the news to him.

You ask what my experience is of the effect on boys and girls of their parents separating. While it is true that no two cases are the same, examples will suggest some of the possible reactions you can expect from Marcus.

Patrick was fifteen. His father was a British diplomat in Africa. Father wrote to the housemaster to tell him that he was separating from Patrick's mother and asked the housemaster to break the news. Parents would telephone a day or two later. I think they were right not to break the news over the telephone from far away. I have had to tell parents living in California that their son had been killed in a climbing accident. I telephoned at 2 a.m. our time in the hope of catching mother and father at home in the early evening. Father answered the telephone. There were animated voices in the background and I had a vision of friends enjoying a drink on the balcony facing the setting sun. Father did not seem able to understand what I was saying; he was elaborately, desperately polite. 'I wonder if you would be kind enough to repeat that, Headmaster?' His wife came on an extension and I had to repeat the news. In the background, the cheerful voices continued for a while and then began to fade as though they were attuned to the parents' fading hope that this was just some terrible misunderstanding.

Perhaps Patrick, too, hoped it was a misunderstanding. The housemaster asked him if he wanted to talk about it. Patrick said no. He had been a happy, open boy with the sort of sunny personality that made him popular with his peers and with the staff. Within a few days of hearing that his parents were separating, he became surly and inarticulate with adults. It was as though he had taken on a different character. He slouched where he had run; he grunted where he had chatted away. Dark clouds covered the sun. He hung about with the most disaffected of his contemporaries. He went out of his way to avoid having to respond to members of staff's greetings. He became careless about his work and off-hand about his commitment to sport (he was a gifted cricketer). It could be that his parents' separation plunged him abruptly into an adolescence that his prolonged boyishness had postponed.

What happens in these cases is that the housemaster pins an envelope on the Common Room board marked: 'For those who teach Patrick —'. Inside there is the simple message: 'Patrick's parents have just separated. He seems to have been particularly hard hit by it. Don't indulge him but please be understanding.' I do not get directly involved because I do not think a boy in this situation wants the headmaster to seek him out and say: 'I am sorry to hear that your parents are separating.' But if an opportunity presents itself I will speak to Marcus because he knows that you are both my friends.

Patrick's work and behaviour went from bad to worse. He was in his O-level year and the good grades that had been predicted looked more and more out of reach. He started smoking, tobacco certainly and possibly cannabis. His frequent breaking of the school rules drove him inevitably into a confrontation with me. On the face of it he was hell-bent on self-destruction. Perhaps he was saying to his parents, 'You may think I have not been hurt but I have and I want to show you how much.' Was it that – a sort of ritualized suicide with expulsion substituting for death? I have known one case and one case only where the boy's response to his parents' separation was to kill himself.

He was sixteen, the only child of talented parents who both had successful careers. They decided to separate as much to pursue their own careers as to escape from each other. The boy was a boarder even though he lived close to the school. He appeared to take the news of his parents' separation calmly. He told his housemaster that it was 'no big deal' and got on with his A-level work. The following weekend he went home. His parents talked over with him the implications of their separation. Knowing the parents as I do, I can imagine the discussion was conducted in a business-like, 'let's-not-get-things-out-of-perspective' manner. No doubt thinking they had dealt with it in a sensible way, the parents went out to dinner, leaving their son, who said he had to finish a history essay. At some point during the evening the boy went into the kitchen carrying a small cushion. He opened the gas stove, placed the cushion inside and lay down with his head on the cushion. Then he turned on the gas. When his parents returned from dinner, they found him dead. In his room, his jacket was over the back of his chair and the finished history essay was on his desk. No note, no message, no word of farewell.

I cannot tell what in a particular case leads from the hurt to the suicide because I do not know. The parents told me that they were sure their son had not intended to kill himself. It was a cry for attention and they would never forgive themselves for being later back from dinner than they had told him. It was, father assured me, 'a gesture, a grand gesture'.

Thank God such 'gestures' are rare. They are at the extreme of the spectrum of reactions to parental separation. Patrick's reaction was close to the middle of the spectrum. With him, my problem as headmaster was that I was damned if I was going to expel him just to satisfy his death wish, yet his offences made it increasingly difficult to avoid doing so. The normal roles of headmaster and naughty pupil were reversed: he determined to make me act in conformity with his wishes and I using every ruse to keep my freedom of action. He could have forced the issue if he had wanted to. It is not difficult to get expelled. But Patrick was intent on going as close to the edge as possible. I do not think he really wanted to go over. The school absorbed his anger and frustration until the end of term. His parents came back to England for the holidays and his mother bought a flat in London. The following term, Patrick was no angel; his angelic days were over. But gradually his hostility to adults thawed. He was wary but not surly. In the sixth form he rediscovered some of his old relish for intellectual challenge, and won a place at Cambridge. He now works for an American bank in New York.

They survive. If I sound surprised it is because I grew up in a family that seemed as secure as it was possible for a family to be. If my parents had separated I do not know how I would have reacted. My surly adolescent days were as sour and self-destructive as Patrick's but had no domestic insecurity to trigger them. I guess Patrick's developing personality had been waiting for an excuse to throw off the eager boy and adopt the manners of his contemporaries but it is impossible to tell how much, if at all, his parents' separation intensified the storms of adolescence.

Popular theory has it that separation means behaviour problems. So it does sometimes; the cause and effect could hardly be clearer. But it is not always the case. Some children of separated parents actually seem to behave better, as though, being vulnerable, they have to tread especially carefully. And of course there are plenty of behaviour problems with pupils whose parents' relationship shows no sign of breaking. I have from time to time done an analysis of those boys and girls who have got into serious trouble. It always breaks down almost exactly fifty-fifty between pupils whose parents have separated and those whose parents have not. Incidentally, that school in New York I mentioned earlier, where 50 per cent of the pupils were from single-parent families, had fewer discipline problems than any school I have known. Perhaps it was just a very good school; perhaps the fact that separation was so commonplace reduced its impact on the children.

I wish I could tell you what to expect with Marcus. He may be like Patrick and rush headlong into adolescence. If he does, don't spoil him; you won't buy his understanding with presents and concessions. He needs assurance of your love but he needs the framework of discipline, too, more than ever. Within that framework he will, with any luck, work out his own way of handling the separation. For him it represents not only the breakdown of your marriage but also the breakdown of the natural order of things. For a time he may feel that he has lost his bearings. The fixed points in his life have suddenly been uprooted. The sooner he can know where the new fixed points are, where home is going to be, the better. But his sense of being off balance may continue for several months. And just as people off balance thrash about, so may he. What he wants is to bring stability and order again into his life. He wants things to be predictable as they were in childhood. That is why the break-up of a family hits so hard if it coincides with puberty and adolescence. Just at the time when the physical and emotional certainties of childhood are being undermined, the secure, predictable context of the family is being undermined as well. If you had asked me, I would have said: 'Separate before Marcus reaches puberty or after his eighteenth birthday.' If only relationships could be planned so precisely!

Is Marcus especially vulnerable? At fourteen he is. As an only child he is. When we separated for a while, our children were helped by being able to talk about it with each other.

There was security in numbers. On the other hand, as an only child Marcus has mixed more with adults and he may have developed a degree of maturity or at least of worldliness that will enable him to adjust more easily to your decision. When I was his age, the word 'divorce' was almost literally unspeakable, bearing as it did the overtones of sin. We were very unworldly children.

Let me end on a more optimistic note. I have known boys who seem to have benefitted from their parents' separation or divorce. They have grown in moral stature. They have developed a striking resilience. Far from throwing them off balance, the separation has given them greater confidence. In one case, a particularly bitter separation, with father leaving to live with a woman half his age, had the effect of launching the son's career. The boy was fourteen, Marcus's age. He never looked back: his shyness fell away; his intellect blossomed; he became head of school. His career at university and in the Treasury have been dazzlingly successful and he will probably be the youngest Secretary to the Cabinet since Lloyd George invented the post. What is more, he is happily married with two young children.

Was that always going to happen or did his parents' bitter parting release in him some energy that might otherwise have remained untapped? Was it a question of challenge and response? We can speculate but there won't be an answer. Any more than there is an answer to how much he was hurt by the separation.

When you tell Marcus, don't anticipate any one response either immediately or in the long term. Love him, be as clear as you can about the new fixed points in his life and don't think that once you have told him, the worst is over. I hope very much it will work out for him and for you.

Yours sincerely

JOHN RAE

(It did not work out all right. The following term Marcus ran away from school and refused to come back. Parents agreed that he should go to a tutorial college in London. He commuted between his father's house in Fulham and his mother's flat in Hampstead. He didn't belong in either place. Adrift in more senses than one, he started on cannabis and was a heroin addict at the age of seventeen. Father paid for an expensive 'cure' at a private clinic in the West Country. The last I heard was that Marcus was off heroin but without a regular job. He is twenty-one this year. As far as I can tell he still has no fixed points in his life.)

12

STRINGS AND BRIBES

Dear Professor Cathcart

I nearly sent your letter to the school solicitor but that would have been a bit heavy. Implying that the headmaster takes bribes is a bit heavy, too. That is what you meant, isn't it? What else can this phrase mean: 'No doubt my son would have been given a place if his father had had the foresight to offer the headmaster and his family a holiday in the Gulf?'

I can't take you seriously. Why the Gulf? Perhaps you imagine that because the Arabs are buying up London they are buying their way into our independent schools as well. In your eyes we are tainted because we work in what you call 'the commercial sector'. As for your son, you say: 'He is probably well out of a sector of education that has the morality of the kasbah.' The kasbah! You have Arabs on the brain.

Look, I'm sorry your son did not qualify on the exam. Your anger and disappointment is all the more acute because you did not really want him to try for us in the first place. That's true, isn't it? You have never approved of the commercial sector but you compromised your principles because the local comprehensives were in such a mess. And then your son failed the exam. You feel like a man whose offer to sell his soul to the devil has been turned down. Your frustration and resentment are not difficult to understand but don't use them as an excuse to accuse us of corruption. What your son needs now is a father who will help him find the right school, not a father who is conducting a public campaign to expose the 'morality of the kasbah' in the independent sector.

You refer at the end of your letter to 'possible press interest'. Come off it, Professor. That is what we used to call 'a thinly veiled threat'. And an unconvincing one, too. Your ivory tower is much more remote from Fleet Street than mine, so don't come the provincial mafioso with me. Instead, let *me* make *you* an offer you can't refuse. I have nothing to hide. I will tell you exactly what my experience has been of parents' attempts to influence the selection process whether at school or university. If you think it amounts to bribery and corruption, go ahead and give the information to the press.

I hope we can agree on one thing. Parents' desire to do their best for their children is universal. As parents, we may sometimes get it wrong; we may not always see what is really best for our children. We may confuse our own ambitions with their needs. We may try to rearrange the world in their favour when what they have to learn is to come to terms with the world as it is. We may use our power and influence in a way that helps them less than it satisfies us. But the impulse behind all these actions is natural and in that sense it is beyond criticism. To question the morality of parents who will go to almost any lengths to ensure that their children have a good start in life, is as pointless as questioning the morality of a lioness who defends her cubs.

So whether you like what I am going to tell you or not, remember we are not talking about people who are seeking power and wealth for themselves or who are trying to rig the system to their own advantage. We are talking about parents whose instinct is to give their children a chance to have life in all its fullness. The instinct knows no barriers of class or nationality. In the Soviet Union, party officials use their influence to get their children into the best schools and even more into the best universities. The string pulling and arm twisting used by these Soviet officials is probably less elegant and more unscrupulous than the methods used by parents in this country who are determined to get their children into the best independent schools or the most prestigious universities. But the instinct is exactly the same.

Does it amount to corruption? Let me concentrate not on what I have read about the Soviet Union but what I have experienced as the headmaster of a sought-after independent school in this country.

There is something rather honest about bribery in its purest form. 'Headmaster, I know my son may be a borderline case in your entrance exam. Guarantee him a place and I will put £250,000 in your name in a Swiss Bank Account.' It never happens, of course, and probably just as well. Consider the anguish of having to turn it down. The headmaster's Swiss bank account remains a figment of the imagination, yours and mine. I have been offered much smaller inducements to take a boy into the school including, you will be pleased to know, a holiday in the Gulf. How did you get to hear about that? It was nicely phrased: 'If you are able to help, headmaster, you will find that I am not ungrateful. The weather in the Gulf is delightful at this time of year.'

I didn't accept any of them, not because I am a paragon of virtue but because you just cannot run an entry system that way. In most independent schools the final decision on which boys and girls are admitted is made by the headmaster alone. If he once abuses that power by accepting a personal bribe, the system falls apart and his credibility as well as the school's is destroyed.

I know what you are thinking. There's more than one way to skin a cat and bribery comes in many disguises. The Arabs may try the holiday-in-the-Gulf approach but the British are more subtle. Influence, pressure, strings, friends of the family and all that. Of one thing you can be sure: the school that is in demand is the one that finds it easy to resist temptation. A popular school does not need the implied advantages that are on offer. Nowadays entry to a good school is on academic merit; the marks are what count. I expect that most headmasters wish that it was not that cut and dried. But at least when entry depends on scoring a certain percentage in the entrance exam, it is not so difficult for the headmaster to reject special pleading. To the parents and supporters of an unsuccessful candidate, he can say, 'I'm afraid there is nothing I can do. The places have all been given to candidates who scored higher marks.' Though in theory the headmaster has the power to insist that one more boy is squeezed in, he is unwise to do so in practice unless his colleagues agree that this is a candidate who for one reason or another has not done himself justice in the exam. If a candidate has failed by a substantial margin, the argument against overriding the result is even stronger. It is not in a pupil's interests to be out of his depth academically.

None of which deters the really determined parent. These parents are not much interested in whether their son will sink or swim academically. They believe in the brand name. Eton and Westminster stand for quality like Cartier and Rolls Royce. It is important to give your son the best; if the best is not available you move heaven and earth to make it so.

A few years ago, the son of a very wealthy man failed our entrance exam. It was only a few hours after the result was known that heaven and earth started to move. I was contacted by two members of the Government, a former Prime Minister, a former Secretary of the Cabinet, and a former Head of the Foreign Office, all asking me to take the boy. There were many other advocates but none more persistent than the former Prime Minister who telephoned a number of times, usually at breakfast. He did not seem embarrassed and was clearly eager to demonstrate that he was doing what had been asked of him.

I sense your puritan nostrils twitching, Professor. You have been a local councillor for twenty years, so you know your way round the back streets of human nature. But if you suspect corruption in this case, I think you are wrong. The boy's father was a generous host whose parties were among the most sought after in London. When his son failed to qualify, the most influential guests were asked to help. There was some talk of father moving his millions – or was it billions? – out of the country if he had to send his son to school overseas. 'There could be a run on the pound,' I was told. I didn't take it seriously; it was a touch of high finance to dazzle the cloistered academic. I refused to override the result of the exam. The pound remained steady. The boy went to another school where he was near the top of the form instead of struggling, as he would have done here.

There is, however, one bribe I think I would have accepted if it had been offered. I am clear and precise about the circumstances. It would have to be a bribe to the school and not to me. It would have to be substantial. It would have to be guaranteed not vaguely promised. And the boy concerned would have to be at least capable of holding his own in the classroom. If those conditions were met, I would sell a place if the price was right. Are you shocked? I doubt it. It confirms your view of the commercialism of the independent sector. But you can buy places in the state sector too. You can buy an expensive house in the catchment area of a good comprehensive. At least if the money goes to the school rather than into the property market the other pupils benefit.

Once the boy or girl is in the school the problem of accepting donations or hospitality from parents almost disappears. Dinner parties, visits to the theatre, presents at Christmas, even holidays in the Spanish villa are part of the scenario of a headmaster's life. But you have to be careful. There can never be anything in return. If the son of the owner of the Spanish villa is in trouble or if he fails to get into Cambridge, he cannot receive treatment any different to the other pupils. Yet even as I write those words I know they express an ideal that can never be completely realized. It is not the gifts or the hospitality that make the difference; it is the friendship that may grow out of them. If you are friends with some parents more than others – and I think that is inescapable – then you are likely to take a little more trouble over their children. It is not that you do less than you should for the others but that you do more than you would for the few. But it never goes as far as failing to expel or favouring for promotion or writing a glowing reference that is not deserved.

When the time comes for university entrance, parents' ambitions can again take them close to, but not I think across, the line that divides legitimate pressure from corruption.

Martin had two Bs and a C at A-level. Against our advice, parents insisted that he sat the post-A-level entrance exam for Oxford. He sat the papers in geography and failed to get a place. Parents did not accept the decision. Their son was 'unquestionably Oxford material'. On his father's side, five generations had been at the university. Both father and mother had extensive connections in the political and academic establishments. They used them in a most efficient way. I disliked what they were doing but I could not help admiring the skill with which they marshalled the big guns to lay siege to one Oxford college after another. They even tried Cambridge but the head of the college they approached was too skilled a diplomat. 'I have sent the papers on to our tutor of admissions with as strong a recommendation as it is decent or prudent for a head of house to give.'

It was not long before an Oxford college appeared to be close to surrender. Father told me that if I wrote a letter of support, victory would be assured.

What would you have done? I had no doubt the boy could cope with Oxford but if there was a place going there must have been a hundred and one boys and girls up and down the country who were academically better qualified. I wrote – honestly I hope, reluctantly I know. The boy was given a place. I did not begrudge him his good fortune but I had no doubt that if his parents had not been able to mobilize the

Establishment on his behalf, he would not have gone to Oxford. It was a classic illustration of how power is exercised in Britain.

Before you reach for the telephone to ring the press, consider this. When you wrote that letter accusing me of taking bribes and threatening to tell the newspapers, weren't you doing the same thing as the parents of that boy? You rejected my decision just as they rejected Oxford's. You had no strings to pull so you tried innuendo and 'thinly veiled threats' instead. Even if you did not expect me to surrender, you were determined to wound me as you withdrew. I don't think you are in a position to take a high moral tone.

Nor am I. I have pulled strings for my children, not always wisely. They have survived rather than benefitted from my manipulation of the academic network. Is there a parent anywhere in the world who would not mobilize the gods on behalf of his child if only he knew how?

The line between striving for your children and corruption is not difficult to identify. It cannot be corruption unless someone is corrupted. Schools and universities cannot be corrupted but individuals can. If I persuade someone to do something he knows to be wrong in return for gain, whether in the form of money or honours, I have corrupted him. Cynical though the smile may be that spreads across your face when you read this, I have never come across an instance of corruption in thirty years of working in the independent sector. Commercial we may be; corrupt we are not.

Now that we have both got our righteous indignation off our chests, shall we meet and talk about your son's future? At thirteen, it will not be easy for him to fit into the local comprehensive. You are firmly against boarding. That leaves other independent day schools. I know the headmasters and would be glad to try and persuade them to find a place. Would you like me to do so?

Yours sincerely

JOHN RAE

233

13

THE PARENT AS SUPERGRASS

Dear Mr and Mrs Craig

I sympathize with your dilemma. It is one that all parents will recognize; I faced it, too, when my children were at school. There is no text book answer to the question: do you tell the school all you know or do you remain silent?

If I have understood you correctly, Richard hinted at the existence of some sort of protection racket operating in the school. You questioned him and are convinced that 'something very serious is occurring'. But you are not prepared to tell me what it is or allow me to question Richard myself. I understand your reluctance and do not criticize you for it. When my son was being bullied at school, I knew what was happening but did not inform the school authorities: I was afraid that clumsy handling of the problem would lead to his being victimized even more. I still don't know whether I was right.

One thing you have to consider, therefore, is how far you can trust me to use the information in a way that will protect Richard. At fourteen he is very vulnerable. A second consideration is the need to protect your relationship with him. He made you promise not to tell the school. If you break that promise, will the damage ever be repaired? But against these considerations you have to weigh a third. Is what is happening so serious, particularly in the harm done to individuals, that you cannot remain silent?

You and I both feel a sense of frustration. You cannot understand why the school does not know what is going on; I understand your reluctance to tell me but without your information I am unlikely to get at the truth. You would be surprised how often over the years parents have said, 'I think there is something you ought to know, Headmaster,' but have been unwilling to tell me any detail, particularly any name, that would give me a lead. With what you have told me, I can speak to housemasters and school monitors but in a school of six hundred pupils a racket can operate without senior boys and girls having any inkling of what is going on. The old school hierarchies may have loosened and the segregation of age groups been abandoned but a school monitor, just because he is in that role, may still be cut off from the 'lads'. In Elizabethan England, headmasters in schools such as this employed secret monitors to spy on their fellow pupils. The school, like the country, was a police state. Some pupils may think that description is still apt. But although the headmaster may be autocratic he has to operate in a way that is acceptable to the pupils, the staff and the parents. Public opinion prevents a headmaster from abusing his power.

I want you to understand this because it helps to explain why headmasters sometimes seem so slow to act. There is a limit to the pressure I can put on a boy who may have evidence that will crack a serious case. I cannot use informers – though boys occasionally offer their services. A senior boy came to see me recently to say he was worried about someone selling drugs in the school. I questioned him. At first I thought he knew nothing but then it dawned on me he had information he wanted to trade. It was the time of term when I was discussing with housemasters the choice of new school monitors. This boy wanted to be chosen. He hinted that if he were a school monitor he would be in a much better position to help me deal with the drug problem. I sent him packing. I would not appoint him a school monitor in a month of Sundays. But his proposition was a reminder that in their political and manipulative ambitions many boys are streets ahead of the way parents and teachers perceive them.

A headmaster needs information but he cannot pay for it. I want the information you have; the trouble is I cannot even give you a guarantee that Richard will never discover you have told me or that his own role can be kept secret from his contemporaries. You should never trust a headmaster who gives you such guarantees.

Let us take the problems separately. Once I start an enquiry, Richard is bound to put two and two together. What I suggest is that you should talk to him again. Don't tell him that you have asked my advice. Say that after thinking it over you have decided that what is happening is too serious for the information to be suppressed and that either you or he must tell someone in authority at school. I am not asking you to deceive him. If he gave you the information on the strict understanding that you would not pass it on to the school, you cannot go back on your promise. But try to help him to see that if the protection racket is as serious as you say, it must be stopped.

The second problem is how to protect Richard. Uppermost in his mind is the fear of being exposed as an informer. He knows what happens to informers in the adult world. He knows that no assurances from the police can guarantee protection. He will melodramatize but we shall not understand his dilemma unless we recognize that his fear of reprisal or ostracism is real. So is his loyalty to his fellow pupils. However strongly he may dislike what is going on, he will dislike even more the thought of being disloyal. I should warn you that adult arguments about duty and the public good do not count for much. He will be thinking about the moment he walks into the Junior Common Room and they all know. So the only thing that will weigh with him is the belief that I can be trusted to keep his name out of it. He knows there can be no guarantee. It might help you to know that I would tell no one – not even my deputy or the housemaster – where the information came from. Indeed I would not indicate that it had come from anywhere.

I hope you will persuade Richard that I ought to have the information he gave you. If you do, let us arrange to meet somewhere away from here. Don't write and don't make an appointment to come and see me. Telephone if you would prefer, though I would rather we met face to face so that there can be no possible misunderstanding about the information and how I am going to handle it. Don't lose heart if I tell you that all this cloak and dagger stuff can have its laughable side. I once met a parent for a private talk at a pub in Belgravia only to find it was a favourite haunt of senior boys who, like me, had reckoned it was outside the school's range. Don't worry, I won't make that mistake again.

A parent in a similar position to yourselves once suggested that the school ought to have a telephone number that parents could ring anonymously. It would get round all this difficulty of being identified as the source of information. I rejected the idea. It smacked too much of a police state or one of those appalling theocracies, like Calvin's Geneva, where citizens are encouraged to make anonymous accusations against their neighbours. What sort of morality would I be teaching my pupils if I followed that example? The means a headmaster uses to achieve his ends are as much part of the teaching process as quadratic equations and Greek vocabulary. Informers, secret monitors, and anonymous accusations not only break the long-established rules of the game; they would sour relations within the community in a way that would make good education impossible.

Keeping the more harmful schoolboy vices at bay without using such methods is a problem for a headmaster but not always an unwelcome one. There are times when I do not regret my inability to get at the truth, just as there are times when I refuse to use evidence that is placed in my hands. A mother went into her son's room and found his diary, hidden, in the amateurish way of boys, under a pile of dirty socks. She could not resist reading it. It was a record of a typical sixteen-year-old kicking over the traces. 'Went to the pub with D and L. Afterwards, party in B's room. Sick in showers. Cut first school this morning.' That sort of thing. Mother brought me the diary and wanted me to use it as the basis for a purge of that boarding house. I told her to put the diary back where she had found it as quickly as possible and to forget what she had read. I am not a crusading district attorney and the pupils are not professional hoodlums, just boys growing up. If I can keep them out of serious trouble, I will. If I can prevent the persecution of individuals, I must. But they need time and opportunity to make their mistakes. If I knew everything that was going on in the school, life would be intolerable for them and for me.

From what you have told me, the protection racket is not one of those cases where I would prefer not to have been told. But you can imagine how maddening it is to know so much and no more.

Here are two cases which might help you make your decision: one in which parents entrusted me with information and one in which they did not.

The first concerns drugs. What made it more difficult for the parents in this case was that their son was not a victim or an onlooker, but a participant. They felt so strongly, however, that the boy who was providing the cannabis had to be stopped, that they were willing to put their son's school career at risk. Their son was fourteen. The pusher – and I think that is the right word in this case – was only a year older. As you know I do not distinguish between the user and the pusher; anyone involved in illegal drugs is expelled.

The parents came to see me. While they criticized the school for not having got on to the pusher, they seemed to understand the difficulty of getting information when the punishment was automatic expulsion. They had decided that the only way to prevent more damage being done as the drug ring expanded was to come to me. They were prepared for the possibility that their son might have to leave the school. They knew the name of the pusher and of seven other boys, mostly of their son's age, who had bought cannabis from him.

I sometimes think about those parents, particularly the father. I did not know him well. He said, 'When we sent our son here we did not expect the other boys to be saints but we did expect the school authorities to respond intelligently to a crisis. We leave the matter in your hands.' I wished they had never come. To expel nine boys who were that young was something I could not stomach. Yet the evidence the parents had given me was cast iron. If I did not expel them all I would undermine the stand I had taken so publicly against drugs. And what of *their* son? He did not know his parents had contacted me but they were proposing to tell him at the weekend. What would his feelings be? He would be facing expulsion at the age of fourteen; he would probably think that his parents had betrayed him, and he would be certain that he would lose all his friends.

I did nothing for forty-eight hours except turn the problem over and over in my mind. I did not consult anyone because I did not want anyone to know just how detailed and conclusive the evidence was. Then, in the way these things do, the right course became clear. I summoned the pusher and expelled him. I called a special assembly and told the school that the boy who had been selling drugs had been expelled. I reminded them that that was the punishment for anyone involved in drugs. I did not tell them that I knew the names of the other boys who had bought and used cannabis. As long as they did not know the extent of my knowledge, my uncompromising policy would not be discredited. I telephoned the parents to explain my decision. I told them that it was essential that they should not tell their son that the information had been passed to me. Father listened without comment. Then he said: 'Thank you, Headmaster. We accept your decision. My wife and I had hoped that you might find it possible to take that course.' Shrewd man. I reckon he had worked it out in advance.

You may think that the father was too calculating, but if he had not come forward it is more than likely that a major drugs bust would have resulted in the expulsion of a large number of boys, including his son. He took a risk in coming to me but the risk of remaining silent was greater. Richard is not involved in the protection racket so he is not in danger of being expelled. The risk of your remaining silent is that the racketeers will continue their extortion and the victims continue to pay up.

The other case I was going to tell you about involved a protection racket of sorts. Three boys in the O-level year were 'borrowing' money from new boys and refusing to pay it back. One of the new boys threatened to tell his housemaster. His room was wrecked, his hi-fi broken, his books torn. His housemaster made inquiries but the shutters came down. The extortion continued. Eventually one of the new boys' parents became suspicious. Why was his son always out of pocket? What was he spending his money on? He questioned his son and the boy revealed the nature and extent of the racket. But parents did not tell the school. Another of the new boys, desperate to replace his travelling money to go home at half term, stole a watch and tried to sell it in a local jeweller's shop. The shopkeeper was suspicious and called the police. The rest you can imagine. The whole story came out but at the cost of a young boy driven to theft. His parents had some harsh things to say about the school and I don't blame them. It was many weeks later that I discovered that not one but several of the new boys' parents had been told about the racket by their sons but had been reluctant to pass the information to the school.

Believe me, I do not underestimate the difficulty of your position. Your first duty is to your son. But you have a duty, too, to help me put a stop to what sounds like an unpleasant form of bullying. If you knew that boys were going to pubs or smoking cigarettes in the cafe across the street, I would not expect you to tell me. But bullying, together with drugs and stealing, are surely too serious for you to say, 'This is the school's problem, not ours.'

If you decide that you cannot tell me, I shall understand. Sooner or later I shall get on to the boys responsible, unless as sometimes happens the racket just ceases for no apparent reason.

If you decide to give me the information we will arrange to meet.

Yours sincerely

JOHN RAE

(The parents decided not to tell me. I alerted housemasters that I had heard on the grapevine that some sort of protection racket was operating but no information about it ever came to light. Richard had a successful and untroubled school career so from that point of view his parents must have felt that they had made the right decision.)

14

GOD

Dear Mr and Mrs Huxley

Thank you for your letter. It is not my job to turn boys into Christians. Their faith or lack of it is their business and their parents'. If you want Stephen to become 'a practising Christian', that is your responsibility. My aims in religious education are different.

I cannot even call myself 'a practising Christian', though that is what the school statutes require me to be. I am at best a fellow traveller. I am a deist; I believe in God in the sense that I believe that our life is not just a pointless biological episode, but beyond that I cannot go. I cannot tell you anything about the nature of God. I admire the teaching of Jesus not because I think he was the Son of God but because he gave men hope. To the question, 'Does our life have any meaning?', he gave an answer of brilliant simplicity: 'Yes, it does, if you are prepared to lose it.' In other words, if we can escape our animal nature our life is not just a pointless biological episode. Jesus's originality was to fly in the face of man's instincts; selflessness not self-preservation is our true destiny. If we are capable of loving one another, then maybe we are not doomed.

I find Jesus's insight into man's destiny exciting, but to suggest that he was divine seems to me unnecessary. I am astonished that over the centuries so many intelligent people have subscribed to beliefs that are not only fantastic but have

134

no bearing on whether Jesus was right or wrong. The miraculous doesn't add to the truth of his teaching, it detracts from it.

So you see I am a deist with Christian overtones. I do not regard that as inconsistent with my position as headmaster of a school that was in the sixteenth century a Christian foundation. I respect that foundation but try to remain true to my own beliefs. If that reconciliation is impossible without some element of hypocrisy – sometimes I must lead the school in prayers that express a Christian faith I do not share – then at least I do all I can to make my own position clear to the pupils. When I preach, I do not think they can be in any doubt about my fellow-travelling status.

You say that as far as you can see the school has no policy on religious education and that this accounts for the 'cynical atmosphere that prevails'. You are wrong – I have a policy. What is more it is designed to counter cynicism. It is also designed to counter religious enthusiasm on one hand and apathy on the other. It is utilitarian as well as idealistic.

The utilitarian side serves a number of mundane but not ignoble ends. Compulsory attendance at morning Abbey for pupils of all faiths and none is partly a gesture towards the foundation but it also provides a knowledge of the particular faith that has fashioned European civilization. The fact that British society now embraces a number of faiths does not wipe out a thousand years of history at a stroke. All children need to understand Christianity because it is so clearly interwoven with the cultural and historical environment they are growing up in. How on earth can a young person make sense of the society around him unless he understands something of the religious impulses that helped to create it? The impulses may now be weak but the Christian charge in our literature and arts, in our constitutional monarchy, in our law, indeed in our whole approach to morality, will remain strong for a long time.

Some parents object to my insisting that their children

should attend the daily Abbey service. My answer is that only a Christian service can give them the feel of what the Christian faith is about; no amount of classroom teaching can do that. Jewish, Hindu, Moslem, agnostic and atheist pupils need to understand Christianity, not just to get a pass in Common Entrance Divinity. I am not trying to convert them. Their faith or lack of it is their business; their ability to come to terms with a society whose character is still Christian is my business.

I have no doubt that as Christians you object to my seeing the daily service in this utilitarian light. I understand your objection. If I were a Christian I would be uneasy about forcing so many non-Christian children to take part in a Christian service. As a deist it does not worry me at all. I am against separate Jewish or Moslem assemblies, just as I am against attempts to turn the Christian service into a celebration of the Supreme Being. The Christianity we project needs to be low key, not triumphalist, but if you make the occasion an inter-faith teach-in then from my point of view the whole aim of the exercise is lost. Ironically, it is the deist who maintains a compulsory Christian service while the headmasters who are Christian make attendance voluntary. One advantage of my approach, incidentally, is that it allows the pupils who are Christian to take part in daily worship without feeling pious.

The other utilitarian value of religion in schools is that it can act, in Napoleon's phrase, as 'the cement of the social order'. Its rituals help to underpin the structure of the community. Not long ago the headmistress of a comprehensive school attended our morning service. She watched it all, she told me, with a 'sense of unbelief', by which she meant disapproval. The compulsory attendance, the masters in gowns, the school rising to its feet as the chaplain and I walked in, the monitor reading the lesson – she saw it all as 'the re-enforcement of the hierarchy'. She expected me to protest that she had misinterpreted what she had seen, but I did not. Different forces help to prevent the school community from flying apart and the hierarchy is one of them. The rituals of religion perform the same service for the headmaster as the rituals of Versailles performed for the absolute monarchy of the 'ancien regime'. Why should I pretend otherwise?

Now to an equally utilitarian but more profound aspect of school religion. I see Christianity as an ally in the task of asserting the importance of morality. It is a curious and interesting characteristic of the English that, however superficial their Christian faith, they have never been able to separate their morality from its religious roots. It is something that foreigners dismiss as hypocrisy: 'a nation of consummate cant', as Nietzsche put it. I don't think it's hypocrisy; we don't take our religion seriously enough for that. I think it is realism. The conventions of religion are useful because they support our moral awareness. That may provoke religious enthusiasts and foreign critics alike, but it works. Long after she had lost her religious faith, the novelist George Eliot retained her respect for religious conformity. Mere attendance at church, she believed, was a recognition that there was a spiritual law which helps to 'save us from the slavery of unregulated passion or impulse'.

It is in this sense of a check on the less attractive side of human nature that I think of religion as an ally. When parents choose a school with a religious tradition their instincts are sound. They may not be Christians themselves but they suspect that regular religious observance will help to moderate the natural excesses of youth.

This utilitarian view of religion also helps to moderate religious enthusiasm, which can be such a curse in a school community. The small group of religious enthusiasts under the leadership of an evangelical master is invariably a source of friction. Though they may not intend it, the members of the group project a holier-than-thou message. They criticize the chaplain for his lack of enthusiasm (the headmaster is, of course, beyond redemption), they mark down for conversion the most insecure of their contemporaries, they close their minds under the pretence of opening their hearts, in short they give Christianity a bad name. There is enough turmoil in adolescence without throwing religious enthusiasm into the pot. I like the approach of Dr Keate, the eighteenth-century headmaster of Eton, who, when told that a boy was showing signs of religious excitement, said: 'I'll flog him. It's all conceit. That boy, if he is a bigot now, will sicken of religion and become an infidel when he leaves school.'

You may laugh at Keate or be shocked by him, but remember the impact of certain religious cults on young people in our own time. Adolescents are attracted by a call to absolute commitment especially if it is presented in idealistic terms. It does not follow that the commitment will do lifelong harm. They grow out of it in the way that most Germans who joined the Hitler Youth outgrew the blind loyalty and the beating drum. But some religious cults are more dangerous because their initial hold on young minds is so difficult to break.

You should be very wary of any religious or quasi-religious cult that approaches Stephen. He is one of the stars of his year, he is good looking and he has a trust fund. He is just the sort of young man the unscrupulous cults will target. If he should ever mention that he has met a pleasant young man, fresh out of Oxford, who has invited him to a discussion group at a smart address in Chelsea or Belgravia, with soft drinks for refreshment – make sure he does not go. It is the first innocent move in a trail that leads to the open prison at the cult's community in California or elsewhere.

The key to these religious cults is the idea of an elite. They trap the bright young men and women with one of the oldest temptations: '*You* have been chosen. It is given to very few to have a chance to help the world recognize the true path. *You* are one of the few.' And so on. And to that temptation, another is added at a later stage. 'Give up everything and join us,' or more accurately, 'Join us and give us everything.'

I am bound to add that for one young man, joining a religious cult was the lesser of two evils. He was at Oxford and a regular heroin user. His talent, his life, were going to waste. While on holiday in the United States he joined a religious cult. He was off heroin in a matter of weeks. I don't know how it happened but it is an interesting insight into why some young people become drug addicts. Despite his high intelligence he could see no point in life. He had joined the drug culture in the forlorn hope of finding the truth that eluded him. It was the cult that provided a purpose and an apparently foolproof answer to the question, 'What shall I live for?' Heroin was no longer needed.

At first his parents tried to rescue him. They went to the United States and retained an expensive lawyer. But when they met their son at the cult's headquarters and saw how happy and healthy he was, they were not prepared to take the risk of bringing him back to normal society. Better, they thought, to lose their son to the cult than to risk losing him altogether to an overdose of drugs.

My suspicion of religious cults, indeed of any form of religious elitism, is in contrast to my respect for an individual whose faith inspires in the young, if not faith itself, then at least a desire to know more. The present school chaplain is such an individual. He is more a parish priest than a school chaplain. Teaching theology is not his scene. But he has this quality, which I have met in only a very few Christians, of making you think that there must be something in it after all if it can affect a man's life in this way. I'm not sure how well Stephen knows the chaplain but I hope he will be influenced by him. Example is the only sure way of encouraging the young to think seriously about what it means to be a Christian.

Your letter speaks of 'a lack of Christian leadership in the school'. That is fair comment on me but not on the chaplain.

His leadership is unobtrusive. He is there when he is needed. He is without exception the only person in this place a boy may speak to in confidence and know the confidence will be kept. When I appointed him we came to an understanding: we would always be open with one another but he would be the judge of what I should be told. He would not be the headmaster's poodle or the headmaster's ferret. You say that he fails to give clear instruction in the Christian faith. Clear instruction! His whole life instructs. Do not ask for more than that. If you have not met him yet, you should make a point of doing so.

I do not share the chaplain's faith (as he knows) but I would not do anything to undermine its impact on the school. So when I turn from the utilitarian to the idealistic side of my policy I have to be careful. My ideal is to awaken in the boys and girls a religious restlessness, a desire to travel and explore. I would like to infect them with the virus of doubt and dissatisfaction, not to make them cynics, but so that they will go on journeying all their lives in the hope of finding God. I cannot bear the thought that they will be apathetic or, worse still, that they will settle for the comfortable answers that the Church of England offers. By all means use the Anglican faith as a basis for morality but do not pretend that it brings you any closer to understanding the nature of God. I don't want my pupils to find peace if peace means that they have given up the search. Do you know what I would wish them to say at the end of their lives? 'I haven't found God but I have never ceased to look for him.'

'No wonder a cynical atmosphere prevails' – you do not need to articulate your thought. But I wish I could make you understand that my ideal is the very opposite of cynicism. Call it naive, rather. I believe in the possibility of God, therefore I want to encourage my pupils to seek him. If I were a Benedictine monk I would wish them to experience the joy of believing that the way to find God is through Jesus Christ;

as a deist I wish my pupils to experience the excitement of travelling hopefully. I do not say the Benedictine has the easier task but at least his message is clear. The trouble with my approach is that it is by its very nature open-ended. The risk is not that the pupils will soon abandon the search but that they will not have understood what I was on about in the first place.

I preach my theme nevertheless. I use the Abbey pulpit to teach not Christianity but the hopeful scepticism that characterizes my own life. You may not like it but at least I preach what I believe, not what I think a headmaster ought to be saying. There are one or two members of the staff who share your view that my attitude to religion is deplorable in a headmaster: using Christianity for 'political' ends on one hand and abusing it with my deist philosophy on the other. One of them walked out of the morning service in protest at something I had said. He did it rather well, not slipping out unnoticed but marching to the centre stage and bowing to the altar. It was a piece of religious theatre. The boys who until that point had been day-dreaming or plotting the downfall of the master who took the first period, came back into focus. (Good heavens, surely you don't think they all sit there listening to what the headmaster has to say!) They enjoyed the moment because it made a change from routine and because they could speculate on what my reaction would be. From the pulpit I said, 'Let us pray,' a useful formula for restoring calm. Later that morning I received a long letter from the master justifying his action with the aid of quotations from St Paul. I threw it in the wastepaper basket, not in anger but because the incident was complete in itself and did not need any justification on his part or reaction on mine. It would be stretching a point to say that I welcomed such interruptions, but that incident at least demonstrated that religion was a live issue. It stimulated debate. The master's protest had served my ends as well as his own.

When you sent Stephen here, what did you want from the school in the way of religious education? Did you really want me to make him a Christian or did you, like me, see Christianity as an ally? Bringing up children is difficult enough nowadays and we welcome all the help we can get. That is how most parents of boys and girls here interpret the value of a Christian tradition. They hope some of the more civilizing aspects of Christianity will rub off and they are prepared to see their children confirmed (though the fathers tend to look shifty when the bishop asks, 'Do you renounce the devil?'). What they do not want is that their son should become a prig; and most would be dismayed if he decided to take holy orders. That is not, as one father told me, why he has given his son an expensive education.

I think this worldly approach by parents is sensible. If you want something other-worldly, you must provide it at home. Religious education, in the sense of bringing up children in a particular faith, is a matter for parents.

Yours sincerely

JOHN RAE

15

EMOTIONAL INVOLVEMENT
OF TEACHERS WITH PUPILS

Dear Mr and Mrs Allington

As I promised at our meeting, I have seen Mr Golding and questioned him at some length. I have also seen Christopher and the other two boys who are said to have had a similar experience with Mr Golding. What I will do is to tell you what I think happened and then comment on your statement that this teacher ought to be dismissed.

Mr Golding has for many years invited members of his history sixth to come to his rooms in the evening to go through their essays. It is almost always on a one-to-one basis. It is the sort of time-consuming, individual teaching that probably only a devoted bachelor schoolmaster can offer. At its best it is wonderfully effective not only in academic results but in the stimulus it can give to the young, developing intellect.

Christopher tells me that he has been on three occasions; the other two boys, who like Christopher are just sixteen and scholars, have each been on four. I saw the boys individually and asked whether Mr Golding had made any physical advances. Of course it was difficult for them to answer, particularly because they are loyal to Mr Golding, in Christopher's case fiercely so. Christopher admitted that Mr Golding had on one occasion put his arm 'round my shoulder', but added, 'There's nothing wrong with that.' The other boys agreed that Golding had put his arm round their shoulders when saying goodnight but, like Christopher, strongly denied that there had been any other physical contact. When I asked Christopher whether he thought Mr Golding had developed an 'emotional feeling' for him (I used your phrase), he corrected me by saying, 'Intellectual, not emotional.'

One or two other points from my talks with the boys. It appears that he spends quite a bit of time criticizing aspects of the school he does not like. One of the boys told me that Golding's hold on the Upper School historians is partly the result of his 'rather revolutionary views', which turned out to mean that he took a libertarian line on most issues of school discipline and supported 'his' boys in their conflicts with the school establishment. Nothing sinister about that. Every school has one. Golding's attitude may be annoying, even disloyal, but it does not follow that the armchair radical is corrupting the young.

I spoke to Mr Golding after I had spoken to the boys. That was a mistake. It was clear from the opening exchanges that the boys had given him a detailed account of their interviews with me. It was naive of me not to realize that they would go straight from my study to his rooms. The result was that he came in a mood of righteous indignation.

How well do you know him? He is fifty-two and last year completed a quarter of a century at the school. For the first ten years or so, he lived with his mother in the town, but when his mother died he moved into the rooms he now occupies. I suppose you would say that he is a lonely man in the sense that he has few close friends on the staff, though he is respected as a good teacher of history. He is punctilious in his human relations almost to the point of caricature. I have often thought that his elaborate good manners were a form of mockery. He appears at first sight to be a self-effacing, even timid man but he is both astute in his dealings and extraordinarily tenacious in argument. With his colleagues he lays a trap for the unwary: if they have a brush with him anticipating an easy victory, they find they have become entangled in a complex and exhausting struggle in which emotion is used to great effect and from which it may take hours to escape.

He also uses emotion as a weapon in his determination to retain his pupils' loyalty and affection. But there never has been any evidence – as there was not in Christopher's case – that Golding made homosexual advances to boys. I do not like the precious, hothouse atmosphere he creates with his coterie of bright young historians, but that is not a reason for dismissing him. When I saw him he categorically denied that there was anything unprofessional in his relations with Christopher or with the other boys. He protested in the most courteous terms at my speaking to the boys on the subject. 'I would have thought, if I may say so, Headmaster, that it would have been more consistent with your own keen sense of justice if you had spoken to me first.'

I stuck to practical matters. He should not put his arm round boys. 'I accept your guidance, of course, Headmaster.' A maddening man – intelligent, prim, prickly, selfish in his emotional demands on his pupils, generous in his devotion to their intellectual development. I have no doubt that he is homosexual in the sense that his emotional life – his hopes and fears, his longing and despair – are dependent on his relationship with the boys he teaches. I also have no doubt that he is not a pederast; he has not made or attempted to make physical love to one of those boys. You may ask how I can be so sure. First there is the power of gossip; in a closed community like this it is unlikely that the stuff of scandal would go unremarked for long. Secondly, I think Mr Golding conforms to a type of schoolmaster, familiar to anyone who knows the history of our boarding schools. With all such men, the arm round the shoulder and the locked door are misleading. These men recoil from the idea of physical love, equating it with lust, as something base and ignoble. Their inhibition, whatever its psychological origin, is the safeguard for their pupils.

You say that 'Mr Golding may already have corrupted Christopher', and that 'he is clearly unfit to remain on the staff'. I share any parents' anxiety about the harm that might be done by a teacher's emotional involvement with their son or daughter. But we need to be clear about the nature of the behaviour that makes a teacher 'unfit to remain on the staff'.

Some cases are easy. At my preparatory school, there was a master who seduced a number of boys aged eleven to thirteen. He invited them to his room and persuaded them to engage with him in mutual masturbation. He was dismissed. No problem of definition in his case: he had exploited his position to indulge his sexual appetite. In those days boarding preparatory schools seemed to attract such men; perhaps they still do, though I suspect that today's more open attitude to sex means that the pederast does not go undetected for long. When people regret the passing of Victorian values they should remember that reticence on the subject of sex made life easier for the pederast.

There is no problem either in deciding that a man is 'unfit to remain on the staff' if he has sexual relations with a girl in the school. He may argue that the girl is over sixteen, that they are in love and that his private life is his own business. None of which alters the fact that as a teacher he is in a position of trust in relation to his pupils, whatever their age.

These are the clear-cut cases. But emotional involvement may go a long way without reaching the stage of sexual relations. It is here that the difficulty of defining 'moral unfitness' arises. What should a headmaster do, for example, if he discovers that a member of his staff has written love letters to a pupil? Such things happen. If the letter was emotional but not explicitly erotic I think I would give the teacher a written warning that his action was unprofessional and that any repetition would raise the question of whether he should remain at the school. If the letter was explicitly erotic I should insist that the teacher resign or be dismissed. Though he might appeal to the school governors or to an industrial tribunal, I do not think he would find support. The distinction I would have made would be between a serious professional error of judgment and a conscious attempt to corrupt.

So far we are still on ground where although there may be disagreement about the headmaster's reaction there is no disagreement about the facts. It is much more difficult in cases where there is disagreement about what has happened or is happening in a teacher's emotional involvement with a pupil. Which brings us back to Mr Golding and Christopher.

There is no legal or moral case for dismissing Mr Golding, but how can I deny that I believe that his influence on the boys closest to him could be harmful? That may seem to you a contradiction: surely if a headmaster believes that a teacher's influence could be harmful he must take some action to prevent it. But the harmful elements in Mr Golding's relations with his pupils would not be universally recognized. Nor can they be taken down and used in evidence against him. They are elusive.

Forgive a frivolous aside but it might help to prevent our discussion becoming too solemn. Some years ago, the senior master showed me a history book belonging to one of Mr Golding's pupils. Inside the back cover was written: 'I must warn you, Mr Golding, that your trousers may be taken down and used in evidence against you.'

Boys can and do laugh at Mr Golding. But that only makes the loyalty of his disciples more intense. Like the members of a religious cult, they interpret criticism of their leader as confirmation of his virtue. Of course the world criticizes because the world is stupid and blind.

What I object to in Mr Golding's relations with boys is this. First, he breaks the fundamental rule for an adult's relations with the young, whether the adult is a parent or a teacher: he makes emotional demands. That may sound dogmatic but what I am trying to say is that adults should not make emotional demands of those whose immaturity makes them vulnerable. No doubt as parents we all do it when our children are very young and at that age it does not seem to matter. 'Do you love me?' a mother asks her two-year-old son, or she applies a little gentle blackmail: 'If you don't eat up your food, you don't love me.' It is all part of the wheeler-dealering that we call bringing up children. But if ten or fifteen years later, mother is still asking, 'Do you love me?' and is still applying the blackmail formula, 'If you love me you would never do this or that', then the emotional demand is beginning to sound like – what is the right word? – exploitation. How much more is the element of exploitation present if a teacher makes emotional demands of his or her pupils?

A teacher is bound to care for his pupils otherwise why is he in the business at all? But caring should always stop short of demanding or expecting any emotional response from them. We all find some pupils – girls and boys – more attractive than others and to pretend otherwise would be dishonest, but we cannot and should not expect anything in return. 'To care and not to ask for any response' may seem an impossible ideal but there are teachers who achieve it. W. H. Auden found one in the person of Walter Greatorex, the music master at Gresham's:

> As a person he was what the ideal schoolmaster should be, ready to be a friend and not a beak, to give the adolescent all the comfort and stimulus of a personal relation, without at the same time making any demands for himself in return, a temptation which must assail all those who are capable of attracting and influencing their juniors. He was in the best sense of the word indifferent . . .

To achieve the ideal requires maturity and self-discipline on the part of the teacher. How many teachers are mature? I sometimes wonder. The profession seems to attract more than its share of angular and quirky personalities. Where would our memories of childhood be without them? Could it be that children need to be taught by some nut cases, that they couldn't cope with a teaching force of normal, balanced adults just as it would be difficult for children to cope with perfect parents? Perhaps the children need to encounter some inadequate personalities in the classroom in order to give them confidence that adulthood is not so difficult to achieve after all.

Some inadequate personalities but not too many, and not if their quirkiness leads them to burden their pupils with their hang-ups. Bruno Bettelheim, the famous child psychoanalyst from Chicago, puts it well:

> But the best discipline of all for the child is the self-discipline of the parent and educator. This is the kind of self-discipline that prevents us from acting out on others our own anxieties and needs, certainly not on our children. This discipline permits us to be on their side instead of forcing them to be on ours. For things to work out to our liking, one's personal life should be such that one would wish his child to emulate this life and take it as a model.

My complaint about Mr Golding is not that he is incompetent or uninspiring or idle. He is none of these. It is that he makes emotional demands on his pupils, that he acts out his anxieties and needs on them. What sort of model of adulthood does that present to the boys in whom he inspires such admiration and devotion?

I am worried too that his homosexual view of life, however repressed or controlled, may disorientate the emotional development of the pupils closest to him. That many good teachers of both sexes are sublimated homosexuals no one would seriously question. Indeed their sexual orientation is one reason why they are such good teachers, particularly in their devotion to their pupils. Nor do I think it is remotely true that such teachers inevitably disorientate the sexual interests of their pupils. Many of these 'bachelor' teachers (some of whom are married) aim for and perhaps achieve the ideal that Auden and Bettelheim describe. They manage to combine dedication with indifference. Lucky the pupils who come across such teachers.

But there is a type of homosexual teacher, of which Mr Golding is one, whose homosexuality communicates an attitude to life, and to relations between the sexes in particular, that I think is harmful. It is a subtle influence, all the more appealing to the brighter pupils because it is presented in intellectual terms. It is in contrast to the superficially more shocking but probably less harmful activities of some repressed homosexuals. Ian Fleming's housemaster at Eton regularly paraded the whole house in the nude, claiming that he felt it his duty to ensure that none of his pupils had contracted venereal disease. No doubt as a headmaster I should feel obliged to discourage such zeal for hygiene but not because I believed that anyone was being harmed by it.

The less obvious and less laughable influence of a man like Golding has its origin in his attitude to women and to physical love. I know, because he has told me, that the principal influence in his life was his classics tutor at Cambridge. He only turned to history in part two of the tripos. His classics tutor inspired him with the ideal of Greek love. I am not a classicist and have never read the Platonic dialogues in which the qualities of love are discussed. But it is well known that the participants in the dialogue come to the conclusion that the highest form of love is of men for each other. Because such love is not a step towards procreation, it remains – so its exponents believe – pure and unsullied by lust. It is romantic love not physical love. The advocate of Greek love recoils from the idea of carnal relations which are seen as gross and repulsive.

I hope that is a fair account. If I understood it better, I might be more sympathetic. I do not question that in its most idealistic form, particularly at the time of its revival in Victorian England, Greek love could be innocent, even noble. It inspired two of the greatest schoolmasters of the time, William Cory and Oscar Browning. (Though both were dismissed from Eton, presumably because their love for boys did not remain strictly within the Platonic ideal.)

The ideal of Greek love seems to me to be based on two propositions that neither reason nor experience support. I am sure two men may love each other with the same intensity as a man and a woman, but to suggest that it is the highest form of love is nonsense. Why should it be? And anyone who has found physical love 'gross and repulsive' has been remarkably unlucky. The whole concept of Greek love seems to me to be a dishonest attempt to deny the connection between love and sexual desire.

None of which would matter if I did not think that Christopher was at risk of being influenced by Mr Golding. Not at risk of being subjected to homosexual advances but at risk of being persuaded that Platonic love is an ideal towards which he should aim. In particular, I think it might distort his attitude to women. Behind his perfect manners, Mr Golding treats women as inferiors, too close to nature to inhibit the intellectual world he has created. It is a strange state of mind with heaven knows what psychological origins but it is not uncommon among those who consider themselves the intellectual elite. I don't want Christopher to develop the same prissiness, the same arrogance towards women, the same rejection of physical love that characterizes Mr Golding. Christopher is sixteen. I would rather he had a sexual relationship with a mature woman than a Platonic relationship with Mr Golding, but I can hardly provide the former or be certain of preventing the latter.

So what can we do? Mr Golding cannot be dismissed. He has committed no offence. He has not, like William Cory, written emotional letters to boys. He cannot change his nature. Cory married after he left Eton and had a son of his own but I can't see that happening to Mr Golding. So we must try to detach Christopher from his influence. Christopher will resent our interference and question our motives. It is a risk, but I will talk to him in the same terms as I have written to you, though not until you have had a chance of absorbing the contents of this letter. If it is any consolation, I have had to do this before and despite the explosion of anger on both the boy's part and Mr Golding's, it worked.

Yours sincerely

JOHN RAE

(It worked in this case, too. Christopher did resent my interference. So did Mr Golding. So did the Common Room, who thought Mr Golding was going to be dismissed and closed ranks. The parents of some of the other boys in Mr Golding's coterie wrote to me, outraged that the one member of staff their sons admired should be accused of immorality. But Christopher's parents handled it well, talking through with him the psychological and sexual implications at the beginning of the holidays. They had to endure several days of almost total non-communication and two weeks of cool, edgy relations. But it passed. In his last year at school Christopher clearly asserted his independence of Mr Golding. The latter, for a while, behaved like a jilted lover, refusing to speak to Christopher in class and cutting him in the street. To my great relief, he was shortly after offered and accepted a post to teach Renaissance history at a private college in Vermont. His former pupils organized a farewell dinner at the Athenaeum, to which as headmaster I was invited. It was an extraordinary occasion, with young men from the universities, from the bar and from the City crowding round their revered teacher. Speeches hailed him as the greatest teacher the school had known and put his departure down to the 'failure of mediocrity to recognize genius'. By the end of the evening, several of the young men were in tears. From this apotheosis of Mr Golding I was glad to slip away unnoticed.)

16

GIRLS IN
THE SIXTH FORM

Dear Dr and Mrs Grace

I cannot tell you whether you should encourage Deborah to apply for a place in the sixth form here. I can only tell you what our experience of a mixed sixth form has been and leave you and her to make the decision.

The practice of admitting girls to the sixth forms of traditionally boys' schools is of so recent origin that you should be suspicious of anyone who pronounces it a success or a failure. Marlborough was the first school to break with tradition. In 1968 the headmaster, John Dancy, decided to end the sexual segregation of the school. He hoped that it could be a step towards the social desegregation of the public schools but in this he was disappointed. His more immediate motive he expressed in these words:

> The desire to render permanent the changes that had come over public schools during the previous decade. I mean the jettisoning of most of the remaining barbarities and absurdities . . . I felt that girls would consolidate the liberal position so that the changes were irreversible.

Critics were quick to point out that the motives did not include the interests of the girls; nor were these interests uppermost in the minds of headmasters who decided to follow Dancy's lead. Some of us, particularly if we had daughters of our own, believed that girls' schools had serious academic weaknesses and we wanted to give girls the same academic advantages as boys, but to pretend that this was our principal motive would be a lie.

In the Seventies, between forty and fifty boys' public schools admitted girls to the sixth form. In all these schools the girls are still a minority. Here at Westminster there are sixty girls in a sixth form of about two hundred and forty.

When I came here there were a few pupils from a local girls' school attending sixth form science classes. They arrived and departed in their brown uniforms, not much acknowledged by the boys, not because they were of a different sex but because they did not belong. I decided that if we were going to admit girls to some A-level courses we might as well admit them to all and make them full members of the school. Once that decision had been taken, the demand for places ensured that the number of girls would rise to its present level.

My motives were complex but not, I suspect, unique. I could see that neither girls nor boys were benefitting from a situation where there was only a handful of girls of indeterminate status in the sixth form. As the father of four daughters, I wanted to give girls a better chance. But I am sure that the strongest motive had its roots in my upbringing and schooldays. I blamed the single-sex boarding school for the shyness, awkwardness and incomprehension that characterized my relations with girls long after schooldays had ended. I suspect that the school only exacerbated aspects of my personality, but that did not weaken my determination to destroy the single-sex edifice, to take revenge upon it, while freeing the next generation from its curse. My resolve was strengthened by my dislike of the form that the male ethos took here: affected rather than boorish, the precious male intellectual rather than the clumsy male yob. I am not a scholar and I think there was a touch of inferiority complex in my eagerness to dispel the arrogance created by the combination of high intelligence with physical and emotional immaturity. As far as this school is concerned, the real dynamic for change was what the headmaster believed were the lessons to be learnt from his own history.

Headmistresses are right to point to the confusion, hypocrisy and self-interest that lay behind the boys' schools' sudden discovery of the importance of providing equal educational opportunities for girls. But they are wrong to argue that because the motivation was questionable the provision for girls was bound to be inadequate. Once the girls arrived, the boys' schools had to adapt and did so successfully. The girls themselves cared little about the motives. What mattered to them was the quality of the teaching, not the headmasters' ideals.

There was no discernible opposition within the school. To my surprise, the masters I had most associated with the precious intellectualism took the change most easily in their stride. They just treated the girls the same as the boys. From the girls' point of view it was probably the best approach. They felt secure because they were treated as members of the community with no special rights. Too many of the other masters treated the girls as though they would burst into tears at the raising of an eyebrow and, to the irritation of the boys, were reluctant to punish them. Boys who arrived late for class were ticked off; girls were all but shown to their seats. It settled down, of course, once these masters realized that the girls were just as shrewd as the boys at exploiting weaknesses in the system.

From the start, the girls were almost always called by their Christian names, though one punctilious bachelor insisted on calling them 'Miss —.' The use of Christian names for all pupils then spread through the school so that now it is unusual for surnames to be used in class, even for boys in their first year. The masters' inability to call a girl by her surname did not fool all the girls; as one of them put it to me: 'Only girls and pets have no surname.'

There is no question in my mind about the girls' motivation. They wanted to use our sixth form as a springboard to higher education, particularly to Oxford and Cambridge. They used us rather more clear-headedly than we used them. The attraction was academic excellence not, as headmistresses still insist on believing, the company of boys. As long as girls and their parents are convinced that the boys' schools give a better chance of success at A-level and university entrance, the flow of applicants will continue. But how right are they? How successful in academic terms has the experiment been?

The honest answer is that I do not know. On the face of it, the girls have done well; they have achieved good A-levels and entry to the university of their choice. But there is no way of telling that they would have achieved less if they had stayed at their previous school. I *think* that the teaching, the competition and the higher expectations here help girls to fulfil their potential more effectively than in most girls' schools. Though Deborah's headmistress would hotly dispute the charge, there are still some teachers in girls' schools who are conditioned to think of their pupils becoming nurses rather than doctors, secretaries rather than barristers. What a good boys' school does for the girls, without being conscious of it, is to help sweep away centuries of conditioning about a woman's role in society.

On the other hand, a girl needs confidence and a thick skin to compete in an A-level set of bright boys. There are casualties. Very few girls leave because the pressure is too great, but some do withdraw into themselves and even underachieve, frightened of being labelled blue-stockings or feminists. Boys can be cruel when their privileged position is threatened. But these few cases should not be used to fuel the myth that girls achieve better academic results in a single-sex school. Some girls do, but for most, as for most boys, the key factor is the quality of the teaching; whether the school is mixed or single-sex is irrelevant. This myth, like the other spread by headmistresses, that in mixed schools girls are reluctant to take up 'boys'' subjects such as physics and maths, has been exploded by the experience of almost every other country in the world. Women in other developed countries such as the USA and USSR have no difficulty achieving high standards in all subjects without the aid of single-sex schools.

There are differences in the way in which boys and girls approach A-level work. I teach a mixed set of historians and I find that most girls are more efficient, or at least more methodical: essays are in on time, notes carefully kept, even handwriting is neater and more legible (I have never known a girl with that almost anarchic handwriting that is not uncommon amongst boys). Is it in the girls' nature to be more conscientious and controlled in their work or is it just the way they have been taught in the girls' school? Or is it simply that in a strange environment they are more anxious to please?

Girls appear to be less dependent on the teacher. Far from needing to be spoon-fed (as some critics of girls' schools claim) I have found that they are better working on their own than the boys. If I set an essay and indicate the background reading, the girls will find the books, do the reading and write a competent essay, whereas the boys will almost always fail to find the books let alone read them, and will rely on their ability to re-hash what I have told them in class. Faced with the problem of writing an essay in a week, the girls will plan while the boys leave everything till the last moment. I am expressing the contrast in rather extreme terms but the underlying difference of approach is true.

When it comes to the public exams, however, there is no difference in the results that the boys and girls achieve; or, to put it another way, with both sexes the results are consistent with ability not with the approach to work over the past two years. Does that mean that the boys are more intelligent and therefore do not have to bother with a methodical approach? I do not think it is a matter of intelligence. I think the boys are more confident of their ability to pull it off on the day; perhaps they are more contemptuous of the value of exams. They are also more confident of their chances of getting on in the world despite a misspent youth. If these boys had come from poor homes and knew that everything depended on their hard work, I suspect their approach to A-level would be the same as the girls'. What I have described as the girls' approach to their work was characteristic of pupils of both sexes in the old grammar schools.

The girls arrive with certain academic disadvantages. The most obvious is that most of them have not studied additional maths. Few girls' schools offer this subject, so that girls who wishto take maths at A-level start behind the boys and take a term or so to catch up. I do not accept the popular belief that girls have less natural ability in maths. As far as I can see, their limitations in this subject are entirely due to poor teaching at an early age and to assumptions – in the family and in schools – that girls who are good at maths are freaks. We are so conditioned to think that mathematical prodigies must be male, that when a twelve-year-old girl wins a mathematical scholarship to Oxford, she inspires more sympathy than admiration.

A disadvantage that results from the style rather than from the curriculum of the girls' schools is a reluctance to engage in public argument and discussion, a reluctance that is re-inforced by a fear of being labelled 'bossy', or worse. The boys here have the gift of the gab to an extraordinary degree. It is inconceivable that any of our former pupils is in hell; they must all have talked their way into heaven. When an Oxford or Cambridge don writes, 'His papers were not up to standard but he was so impressive at the interview that we decided to give him a place,' I cannot help reflecting what an advantage it is to be brought up in the sophisticated, urbane society that confers this gift of articulateness on its members.

The gift does not give the boys any advantage in, say, physics, but it does in English literature. Girls are often taken aback by the fluency and gall with which a sixteen-year-old boy will publicly contradict the master's interpretation of the text. But it is upbringing not gender or intelligence that gives him the confidence to do this. When girls acquire that confidence, as most of them do, they have no difficulty holding their own in the classroom debate.

My daughters who came here reckoned that it took girls about a term to adjust to the new environment. Ten years after the first girls arrived, the school remains an overwhelmingly male institution. Towards this unyielding male ethos, the girls are ambivalent. Like a radical elevated to the House of Lords, they are torn between an urge to change the institution out of all recognition and a desire to preserve the privileges they now enjoy. My impression is that the more mature girls adopt an attitude of amused detachment as though they are studying at a foreign university. The local customs and prejudices might intrigue or infuriate, but it is a mistake to take them too much to heart.

If they are at all perceptive, they can learn a lot about the psychology of the opposite sex. Apart from A-level, those two years can be a crash course in the male. It may be argued that a boys' public school is so unlike normal society that girls will need re-educating when they emerge. On the contrary, the boys' public school teaches the girls, in a way that no other institution can, how to survive and succeed in a society where power is still in the hands of men. Though it is early days yet, the signs are that the girls who have been here are successfully making their way in such male-dominated worlds as the City and the Law. Unlike their contemporaries from the single-sex girls' school and from the co-educational comprehensive, they have seen the enemy in his lair and know how to get the better of him.

Not that I imagine the girls arrive here with many illusions about boys. If they do, the illusions are quickly dispelled. Though some headmasters claim that the arrival of girls has made the boys more civilized in their behaviour, my impression is that the reverse has occurred. Less mature, perhaps, and less secure in their own sexuality, the boys tend to become aggressive, either in harmless but eye-catching macho displays, or in the sort of spiteful comments men associate with femininity. There are deliberate attempts to keep the girls in their place. At one of the big country boarding schools which has admitted girls, the 'lads' award the girls marks out of ten for sex appeal; as the girls walk out of the dining hall, they have to run the gauntlet of shouts of 'six', 'eight', 'three' and so on. Those boys would have been dismayed to learn that their own sex appeal was being even more clinically assessed. Not long ago, the clerk of works showed me a wall covered with graffiti in the girls' lavatory. Most of the comments were on the physical attributes, or lack of them, of both masters and boys.

The British have for so long been convinced of the virtues of single-sex schooling that they find it difficult to dissociate the idea of a mixed school from the idea of progressive – and by implication permissive – education. Girls and boys in the same school seems only one step away from boys and girls in the same bed. Yet I am not aware of any evidence that links the type of school with the sexual morality of the young. If young people are more likely than in the past to have sexual relations before marriage, that change in social mores does not appear to have any connection with whether the schools they have attended were co-educational or single-sex. This is worth emphasizing because there are still those who imply, even if they do not state it openly, that the mixed sixth form makes sexual relations more likely.

The experience of the boys' schools that have admitted girls to the sixth form suggests that the reverse is the case. In a boarding school, where the rules make it clear that a boy and girl found in bed together will be expelled, sexual relations are not a course easily open to the pupils. Expulsions under this rule have occurred, it is true – I know of a headmaster who expelled his own son for being in a girls' dormitory, not in anyone's bed – but the few exceptions prove the rule. What the pupils do in the holidays or the day-pupils do away from the school, is not within the school's knowledge or control.

It is a fair comment that headmasters and headmistresses are among the last people to be well informed about the sexual activity of their pupils and it would be naive to suggest that sixth form pupils could not have sexual relations without the authorities' knowledge. What I am arguing is that there is nothing in the nature of the mixed sixth form that makes this more likely to happen. Boys and girls do make close, sometimes intense relationships. It would be very odd if this were not the case. But it is not easy for them to develop such relationships in the public arena of a school campus. Their contemporaries are more watchful than the authorities. Some schools impose rules to keep the sexes apart: a six-inch rule in one school, a ban on PDA in another. (You may well wonder, as I did, what PDA is; it stands for Public Displays of Affection.) We have never introduced such rules because they would be laughed out of court. And are public displays of affection so undesirable?

The received wisdom is that girls at sixteen are more mature emotionally than boys, and it is a generalization that I accept. Certainly, the girls here are more single-minded in their determination not to be distracted from their academic goals. They enjoy having friends who are boys and not being in a single-sex society where the obsession is with boyfriends. Paradoxical as it may seem to the headmistress, the mixed sixth form helps girls to get boys off their minds. The fact that the behaviour of some boys in their year is immature helps the girls to distance themselves from emotional entanglements that would get in the way of their ambition. If they do find themselves emotionally attracted, it is not infrequently to one of those boys who, in the headmaster's eyes, are the most villainous and decadent. You will think it sexist of me to say so, but the attraction of amorality is as powerful in a seventeen-year-old boy as it is in any wicked hero of a romantic novel.

In vain, headmasters hope that the most balanced girls will be attracted to the clean-living and responsible members of the school establishment.

Though some of them may be attracted by the rogues, the girls themselves are not much involved in crime. They smoke as much as the boys, drink less and are much less likely to be involved with drugs. On the other hand they pay only the most cursory attention to the dress regulations and are rather worse than the boys at turning up on time, particularly to school occasions such as morning service in the Abbey. If the boys' attitude to the routine regulations is often cavalier, some girls refuse to take such regulations seriously. Not having been brought up in the ways of a boys' school they do not look upon the conflict between freedom and authority as a game (British prisoners of war and basically decent if incompetent German guards) nor do they find it easy to attempt the argument that abiding by the rules may be for 'the good of the school'. Appeals to their loyalty to the institution are not so much rejected as not understood. There are exceptions, of course, girl school monitors and one girl head of school, who not only understand but have the political nous to interpret their understanding to their contemporaries.

Critics of those boys' schools that have admitted girls to the sixth form claim that the policy is not in the best interests of the girls, but regardless of what the school's original motive may have been, our experience suggests that it is very much in their interests, as long as they have the toughness and maturity to handle the academic and social pressure.

But what of the boys? Is it in their best interests to introduce a small number of girls into their privileged, male world at the high noon of adolescence? What confusions, what heartaches, distract them from the serious business of being successful? Nothing I have observed or remember from my own adolescence persuades me that the distractions of reality are any more potent than the distractions of fantasy. In other words, the girl sitting next to you in the classroom is no greater distraction than the girl who haunts your imagination. At sixteen I wrote love poems to imaginary girls during history lessons; if it had been a mixed sixth form I would probably have concentrated more on the French Revolution.

The boys' A-level results have improved every year since the girls arrived. I do not suggest that is cause and effect, though the girls have provided more competition; but the results refute any suggestion that in the mixed sixth form the boys are distracted from their academic work.

But on what was for me the crucial, starting point, that is whether the boys have a better chance than I did to lay the basis for mature relationships with the opposite sex, I am an agnostic. I just do not know how far the experience of the mixed sixth form improves that chance. All I can say is I hope it does.

I suggest that you show this letter to Deborah. If it puts her off, do not try to change her mind. If she is encouraged, talk through with her how she would cope with the various pressures: the academic whizz-kids waiting to snipe at anything she says in class; the moody, adolescent boys who refuse to talk to her at lunch; the rudeness and the language that is intended to shock or diminish her; the soulful gaze of the inarticulate admirer; and the condescending attitude of some of the staff. Nothing, perhaps, that a level head and a sense of humour cannot handle.

If she still wishes to go ahead, the next step is for her to spend a morning at the school later this term. I will arrange for one of the girls to look after her; she will take her in to lessons and lunch. That way Deborah will have a chance to talk with other girls and boys, and to get some feel of the atmosphere. It will be interesting for her to compare what I have written with what the girls tell her.

Yours sincerely

JOHN RAE

17

REPORTS

Dear Dr Rae

I am writing because I just do not know how to react to Andrew's report. Not for the first time, I found it very depressing. It is like receiving a large income tax demand you knew was due but which came as an unpleasant surprise all the same. The report arrived this morning. As so often happens, Andrew's father left for the office as soon as he saw the envelope.

I read each report out loud to Andrew. Was that wrong? Perhaps I should have let him read them first. He just shrugged his shoulders or made excuses. All his friends, according to Andrew, have had bad reports this term because you told the masters to 'get tough' with the O-level year. If that is true, don't you think parents ought to have been warned?

Mr Kruger says that Andrew will fail O-level maths unless he 'finds the motivation to work without delay'. He doesn't say where Andrew is supposed to find the motivation. I am tempted to write to Mr Kruger to tell him that motivating Andrew is what he is paid to do. I don't understand Dr Peterson's history report. I am sure it is very clever to write that Andrew should remember that even Pope Pius IX was not infallible, but that doesn't explain to me why Andrew is apparently so complacent about passing the exam. The housemaster's report says little about Andrew's work. The main complaint is that the French master (whose name I cannot decipher) says that his attitude has been 'slightly frivolous this term'. No doubt that is reprehensible in a sixteen-year-old on the verge of O-level but the housemaster's comment – 'I was extremely upset to read this reference to frivolity' – just made Andrew laugh and I cannot blame him. To be honest, your headmaster's report was equally unhelpful. For £6000 a year, I could have told you that Andrew 'will have to work harder than this if he is to realize his potential'.

I am particularly angry that the reports bear so little relation to what I was told at the parents' meeting earlier this term. It is bad enough to have to stand in those interminable queues but when you do at last reach the teacher you expect to be told the truth.

I am sorry to put it so bluntly, but unless I know how seriously the school regards these reports, and whether I am to take them at their face value or as some sort of coded message, I have no idea whether I should take a firm line with Andrew or shrug them off as lightly as he does.

Yours sincerely

Barbara Rogerson

* * *

Dear Mrs Rogerson

Thank you for your letter. I think the best thing I can do is to tell you something about the way in which these reports are written. It won't answer all your questions, but it may help you to interpret the message they contain.

Reports are one of the few formal and regular communications between school and parents. Unlike the teachers' comments at parents' meetings, reports have something of the authority of a historical document. It is easy to argue that someone did not mean what he said, not so easy if the written evidence is in front of you. But like historical documents, reports are no more true or accurate than the writer was able or willing to make them. So I think your response should be serious but not solemn. Their judgements are provisional, not absolute.

Schools write reports for the obvious reason that they want parents to have an up-to-date assessment of how their son or daughter is getting on. They also have less obvious reasons: they want to cover themselves if something goes wrong – 'We did warn you that he might fail' – and to assure you (and me) that it is not only the pupils who have done a good term's work.

I think the quality of the reports is a gauge of the school's professionalism. Some schools don't write them. Is that laziness or a misguided egalitarian belief that reports, like form orders, encourage competition and make some children think they have failed? If my child is at school, whether private or maintained, I want to know how he is doing and I expect the professional to be prepared to commit his opinion to paper. I accept that the necessity of writing a report every term can encourage teachers to use bland clichés, but the whole point of regular reporting is to give those teachers who have got something important to say the opportunity of doing so. In that sense some reports are in code and parents need to distinguish the routine comment from the authentic attempt to provide them with an insight into their child's progress.

That is why the headmaster's reports so often appear limited. In the majority of cases a word of encouragement, congratulation or warning is all I can write. I do not know the pupils well enough to do more. But there are always a few cases when I know that I must write a particular message to the individual. Those few reports justify the system.

One pupil at least shares your view of the headmaster's reports. I don't know who he is but he sent me postcards from all over North America, reporting on his trip in the stock phrases I use. 'San Francisco has made a good start'; 'Vancouver has yet to realize its potential'; 'My best wishes for

Calgary's future' and so on. The joke wore thin by the time he reached Toronto but he had made his point.

Reports are written under pressure in the final weeks of term, and under pressure the quality varies. What is written not only reflects the writer's professionalism, but also, of course, his personality. Reports that look obscure to parents can be revealing to anyone who knows the author; and they are one way in which a headmaster can assess his staff.

Despite what you say, I think the standard of report writing here is high. Most members of staff take a lot of trouble and the number of coded clichés is surprisingly small. Only very occasionally do I have to send a report back to be re-written because it has crossed the line between professional assessment and personal abuse. 'I find his attitude negative and sometimes rude', is a professional assessment; 'He is the most unpleasant boy I have ever had the misfortune to teach', is personal abuse.

Professionalism should prevent teachers using the report as a means of getting their own back on the pupils. 'His sour demeanour has all but poisoned the atmosphere in this set', is a strong criticism of a sixteen-year-old boy, but is it fair comment or the teacher's dislike of a particular pupil? Should the headmaster and parents take it seriously or just as a coded message that teacher and pupil get on one another's nerves? I knew the answer because I knew the teacher. He was a mature and balanced professional, not given to exaggeration. I discussed the boy with him and was in no doubt that the report should stand, though I asked the housemaster to tell the parents that the report should be taken at its face value.

The secret of the correct interpretation of reports lies in the closeness of the relationship between the parents and the school. If the parents know the teachers well and can rely on the housemaster to interpret for them where necessary, there should be little difficulty in making sense of reports. My first thought on reading your letter was to wonder why you had not spoken to Andrew's housemaster; you may not like what he has written but he could have helped you interpret the other reports.

The interpretation of reports is made more difficult by the individual teacher's desire to present himself in a good light, particularly to his colleagues and to his headmaster. He may, for example, exaggerate the amount of work he has covered with the class or play down the discipline problems he is having. I remember a fairly senior master who made a point of emphasizing in his reports that he never had any difficulty with the boys who were 'clearly causing so much trouble to my colleagues'. It wasn't true but he managed to build a reputation as a disciplinarian both with his colleagues and with parents. It was a skilful use of reports as a medium of public relations or, rather, disinformation.

In a similar case, a teacher who was being given a very rough time by a group of fifteen-year-olds, wrote each of them a very favourable report. Why should he do that? Perhaps he wanted to appease the angry god of adolescence and imagined the boys thinking of him as 'not a bad sort really'; or perhaps he wanted to persuade himself that he was in command of the situation and could afford to be generous.

Sometimes a teacher's undisclosed motive can have a happy effect. I knew a master who so much wanted to be liked by his pupils – and don't we all – that he always ended his reports with the same phrase: 'He is a great pleasure to teach'. Maybe it was not true in all cases but it meant that even the bad reports ended on an up-beat. The parents knew that he used the same phrase about every boy but they appreciated the fact that going through the reports was less traumatic; however depressing the picture that was unfolding, they knew that the friendly phrase was waiting to welcome them.

A final variation on this theme is the teacher whose enthusiastic reports are part of his recruiting campaign. When, for example, boys are making A-level choices, a teacher who is keen to persuade the bright boys to choose his subject may exaggerate the boy's prospects. Comments such as, 'There is no doubt he has a great future in this subject' should be treated with caution. Reports always tell the truth. The problem for parents is to know whether it is the truth about the pupil or the truth about the teacher – or both.

There is a way round the problem of interpretation. At Eton, together with reports parents receive a letter from the housemaster, summarizing and interpreting the opinions of his colleagues. That is a sensible idea and if it is not more widely used it is because teachers feel that their status is in some way diminished if someone else is interpreting what they have to say.

You asked me some specific questions.

It is not true that every boy in the O-level year has had a bad report; Andrew is only using the most commonplace of schoolboy excuses, safety in numbers: 'Nobody does Mr Smith's prep'; 'Everybody breaks that rule.' Nor have I told the staff to 'get tough' with the O-level year; that is a master using me as an excuse for turning the screw. But I do from time to time have to remind the common room that it is their job to make the boys work; an obvious point, you might think, but like you I am sometimes exasperated by colleagues who tell me that the boys in their form are not working hard enough. Most adolescent boys will do as little work as they can get away with; they only dimly sense that it might be in their interests to do more. It is therefore up to the master to demand more and better work. Boys are pragmatic; they don't object to hard work on principle; they just don't see the point of exerting themselves unless they have to. For all the elevated educational theories about the importance of pupils discovering things for themselves, when you are fifteen or sixteen you need a demanding teacher who will insist that you discover the answers whether you like it or not. That requires stamina and energy on the part of the teacher – the more work you set, the more you have to mark – and some teachers don't have enough of either. When Mr Kruger and I say that Andrew should work harder, you are right to throw the comment back at us. I do not think I have ever known a master write: 'I have failed to make him work hard enough', but it *is* our job. What we would like is your support.

Dr Peterson's history reports are collector's items. His doctoral thesis was on the papacy in the nineteenth century and his reports have always contained obscure allusions to the period. I have never thought to tell him not to do it. Reports are dull enough without proscribing the last remaining idiosyncrasies. As for the French master, Mr Duprée, I don't think he intended anything more than a mild rebuke and the housemaster took it too seriously. Adults should never admit to being 'extremely upset' by the antics of the young, should they? It sounds so peevish. And when he is 'extremely upset' by 'a slightly frivolous attitude', how will he react if Andrew sets fire to the house matron?

Parents' meetings! They are a necessary burden. With six children I have suffered longer and harder than you. Some useful information is exchanged and it must be helpful, for the reasons I have given, for the parents and teachers to know a little more about each other. But these occasions seem to have been designed to bring out the worst in the participants. In the queue, I am as impatient as you are; the parents in front of me invariably have brighter children and chatter away to the teacher as if no one else were waiting. When it is my turn, I want to get away as quickly and lightly as possible but the teacher, with singular insensitivity, appears to enjoy exploring my children's shortcomings.

It is a struggle for supremacy, you know, this face to face between parent and teacher. The parent is paying the teacher's salary one way or another and is damned if he is going to be treated like a naughty schoolboy; the teacher holds the child's future in his hands and is damned if he is going to be treated like a hired servant. In this struggle the teachers do not usually pull their punches; on the contrary I suspect they enjoy relaying the bad news. So I am surprised and sorry that they gave you too optimistic a picture of Andrew. Yet for some pupils it is all worth while and, as in the case of reports, it is those cases that justify the system.

You ask my advice on how to go through the reports with Andrew. You should have let him read them first. I shouldn't worry too much that his father opts out of the first shock. It is not uncommon for one parent to take this responsibility; there is something to be said for the initial discussion to be on a one-to-one basis. But I hope Andrew's father will read the reports and support you in whatever line you are taking.

I wouldn't worry either if Andrew's first response is to shrug off the criticism. Give him time. The beginning of the holidays can be a no man's land for children, particularly if they have been at boarding school. They are not sure whether they are glad to be home or not. Andrew doesn't want to talk about his reports, not just because they are bad but because they are a reminder that the two worlds he has managed to keep apart are really in collusion with one another.

But don't let him get away with it altogether. There will come a point after a week or so, when you will know that it is time to ask him if he has been set any revision to do during the holidays. He'll probably get down to it with an efficiency that will surprise you: clearing his desk, sharpening his pencils, ringing up his friends to borrow their history notes. After that first flourish, which may last all of half an hour, his spirits will sag. Then he will need your support. I wish there was a formula for encouraging our children to work. It is maddening that they will not take our advice but I recall a merchant banker telling me that companies in trouble never took his advice until six months later when the situation was much worse. I am afraid the situation may have to get worse before Andrew takes the advice we are all giving him now. It is difficult to resist trying to accelerate the process, particularly with an exam in a few months' time, but I would be patient if I were you. 'All you ever talk about is work!' shouted our fifteen-year-old daughter as she slammed the door and took off for one of her schoolfriends' homes for the night. But don't despair. There will be many false starts before Andrew learns to motivate himself, and quite a few slammed doors and midnight wanderings. Just stay with it. 'He was never in the way and never out of the way,' was how people described Marlborough's political ally, Sidney Godolphin. That is the sort of ally Andrew needs you to be. The trouble I found when my children were Andrew's age was that I so often got it wrong. I was too much in the way when the last thing they needed was my nagging them about work; and too much out of the way when their confidence badly needed my encouragement. And I almost always spoke off the cuff, believing that as a headmaster I was bound to get it right. At least you will not make that mistake.

Yours sincerely

JOHN RAE

18

LATE DEVELOPERS

Dear Mr and Mrs Turberville

Yes, I do believe in the late developer. I know he exists. So I am angry that Mr Porter should have used that phrase on Duncan's report. It sums up all that I dislike about the academic cast of mind. I remember a similar remark made by a headmaster, a double-first-in-classics man whose lofty manner signalled his contempt for anyone not in his class. 'The myth of the late developer', he told the annual meeting of the Headmasters' Conference, 'is the last refuge of parents with stupid children.' That is academic arrogance at its worst.

You will gather that I find it difficult to be dispassionate on this subject. My own experience colours my judgement. I failed A-level, or Higher Certificate as it was then called. When I applied to Cambridge I was advised to go straight into commerce. When I started teaching, the headmaster asked if I would like to take a non-academic role as head of physical education. Only when I approached London University to do a doctorate did anyone take me seriously. The professor to whom I was assigned just assumed I was capable of doing the research; I had no choice but to live up to his expectations.

It is a commonplace story and not at all remarkable, yet there are still many teachers and academics who write off children because they have not passed the right exam at the right age. The late developer is unpopular and must be kept in his place. He threatens the authority of those who wish to put children into watertight categories; he calls into question the credibility of academic qualifications; he casts doubt on the school's judgement. In short, he is subversive.

But it is not just personal experience. I am increasingly convinced that education in this country is designed to prevent the majority of children developing their potential. There is an unholy alliance of elitists and egalitarians who unwittingly join forces to restrict opportunity to a small minority. The elitists think that only a minority are worth educating beyond the age of sixteen; the egalitarians try to hold talent back because they believe it is divisive. What madness! So much talent wasted. So much promise unfulfilled. It is almost as if our society is so afraid of the potential of its people that access to opportunity has to be strictly controlled. In other countries a well-educated population is regarded as a source of strength; in Britain it is feared as a source of social unrest. If I believe passionately in anything, it is in the need to break this stranglehold that the academic establishment and its egalitarian allies have on the young of this country.

Before I talk about Duncan, I ought to define my terms. What exactly is a late developer? Strictly speaking he (or she) is the opposite of an infant prodigy, Mozart's distant mirror, a person whose talent flowers late. But that definition begs a question. Would the talent have flowered earlier if the circumstances had been favourable? Nothing, we suspect, could have prevented Mozart's talent bursting forth but with the late developer it is not always clear whether the talent *had* to take a long time maturing or some discouragement and disadvantage in youth caused the delay.

With the late flowering of academic talent it is almost always the latter. The extent to which teachers undermine children's confidence is alarming. Parents do it too. Wishing to protect their children or themselves from embarrassment, they say, 'John will never make an artist', or 'John is no good with his hands', and every time the phrase is repeated it reinforces the child's mental paralysis. Innocently and unintentionally, the doors of possibility are screwed up.

This is particularly true in subjects that are thought to require innate ability, such as mathematics and languages. 'John will never make a mathematician', is all too familiar whereas 'John will never be any good at history' is not, because in history hard work rather than innate talent is seen as the key to success. There *are* individuals who are born with an aptitude for mathematics or languages but it does not follow that almost everyone else will find the subject difficult. People who are 'hopeless with figures' can make remarkably swift calculations if money is involved, and very few people fail to learn a foreign language when circumstances force them to do so. It is only the education system that sets low targets for the development of the individual's potential in these subjects.

For far too many children, confidence is undermined, not in one or two subjects, but across the board. They leave school at sixteen with few or no qualifications. Only the lucky ones get a second chance.

David left school with no qualifications. He became an unskilled labourer, digging the tunnel for the Victoria Line. As far as his teachers were concerned, he lived up – or down – to their expectations; he had no academic potential, his intelligence, such as it was, pointed at best to a career as a semi-skilled worker. Today, at the age of thirty-five, David has an MA and Ph.D. in history and is a lecturer in trade union history in higher education. In terms of academic achievement he is streets ahead of the teachers who wrote him off at the age of sixteen.

In David's case, the catalysts appear to have been his marriage to a teacher and his awakening interest in trade union history. Encouraged by his wife, he studied for A-levels in the evenings and won a place at Warwick University as a mature student. From there he never looked back.

Jane left school at sixteen with no O-levels and only two

CSEs. She worked for some years as a shop assistant in a chain store. I do not know what the catalyst was for her but in her late twenties she started to study in the evenings and won a place at Lucy Cavendish College, Cambridge, which was founded to enable mature women to return to full-time education. She now has a degree in law and is a practising solicitor.

Those are true stories. Were their schools negligent in not diagnosing ability? That may be a harsh judgement but you can imagine the outcry if a doctor fails to diagnose a serious illness. Of course, potential is not as easy to diagnose, particularly when it has been buried deep by early discouragement. And even the best teachers cannot always recognize the quality of character that we might call the will to achieve. In the case of David and Jane, the ability to achieve what they did was always there as I believe it is in many others who never rise above the judgement of the school system. What David and Jane had was the will to achieve and the opportunity to do so.

With another sort of late developer – the man or woman who reveals unexpected talent that has little or nothing to do with academic ability – the catalyst sometimes has to be a major social upheaval that shatters the existing rules. My favourite historical illustration is André Masséna.

Masséna retired from the French army in August 1789 with the rank of company sergeant-major and set up a shop to sell dried fruit. To all intents and purposes he was just another ex-soldier, unfit for high command and unlikely to make more than a modest living. The French Revolution and Napoleon changed the rules. Masséna became one of Napoleon's leading marshals, a duke and a rich man. When he died he left a fortune of forty million francs. The ability was always there; what it needed was the catalyst and the will to achieve. Look around you on the bus and in the street. If a revolution changed the rules in Britain, it would surprise you which people would be catapulted to prominence.

You could hardly blame a school for not spotting Masséna's military talent. There are types of intelligence that schools cannot measure. I remember a boy who left without a single A-level pass, a failure in this school's terms. Ten years later he is a successful restaurateur and entrepreneur. Such people are late developers in a different sense from André Masséna. He was held back by the rigid social structure of French society before the Revolution. The restaurateur was not held back. His type of intelligence did not register on the academic scale. His talent had no reason to blossom in the academic environment.

The school system measures and praises a certain type of intelligence. Intelligence tests measure verbal and logical reasoning ability. That is an important type of intelligence but there are many others that the tests are not designed to measure. They do not measure the intelligence required to assemble a car engine, to bring up a child, to run a successful business, to command an army. Nor can they measure common sense. There is no harm in this as long as teachers and parents do not believe that verbal and logical reasoning is a superior type of intelligence. Unfortunately that is exactly the message that the academic rat-race emphasizes. Duncan's academic malaise is partly a revolt against that emphasis.

The emphasis on one superior type of intelligence is also what turns off many pupils in the maintained schools. The tragedy – and it is not too strong a word – is that many never discover what their potential is. These young people are the victims of a society's conspiracy to keep them in their place. When I was visiting a comprehensive school in North London, a teacher told me that he did not insist that his O-level pupils did prep because to insist was 'too directional'. I told him that by failing to insist on homework he was part of a conspiracy to keep the working class in their place. He was not amused. Who was I, the headmaster of an elitist school, to criticize his educational philosophy? He could not see that the elitist school and the voluntary prep were different facets of the same conspiracy. Elitists and egalitarians both work towards the same end.

Duncan is not the victim of a conspiracy except in the sense that he is rebelling against his good fortune. 'His change from intellectual energy to almost complete apathy', his housemaster writes, 'is not unknown at his age, but he has joined the counter-culture with a vengeance.' It is strange how this adolescent disaffection hits some boys harder than others and some boys not at all. Don't ask me why this is. Some boys shrug it off in a few months; some do not rediscover a sense of direction for several years. The system requires them to peak academically at eighteen but maturity will not be hurried.

The hiatus in Duncan's will to achieve is, I think, due to natural causes, in which case it is neither permanent nor damaging. He has not suffered from any of the various disadvantages that can stop other children in their tracks. My guess is that by the autumn he will be determined to start moving forward again. It will probably have nothing to do with exhortations from me or from you. Autumn is the start of the football season. Duncan loves football and respects the master in charge. As the same master will be taking him for A-level history, Duncan will be able to rationalize to himself the reawakening of his enthusiasm for that subject. On such chance encounters so much in education depends.

If I am wrong and Duncan fails A-levels or produces grades that have little value in the market, that will be a cause for disappointment but not despair. He has potential but it may take longer for him to discover what that potential is and how to develop it. Whatever happens, believe in him.

Yours sincerely

JOHN RAE

(Duncan's parents could not refrain from pushing him. A bitter argument ended with Duncan shouting at his father,

'Come the revolution, you'll be done away with.' His father turned him out of the house. Duncan went to live with the family of a schoolfriend. He threatened to leave school altogether but the attraction of football was too strong. As luck would have it he was injured for most of the season and his relationship with the master he respected never developed. He passed two A-levels at modest grades. He refused to retake the third exam at a tutorial but agreed to his father's suggestion that he spend a year working in Australia. The former Empire still soaks up some of the growing-pains of England's young men. Duncan spent the year working on a sheep farmer's property at Wogga Wogga in New South Wales. He came back last year, still determined not to pursue his academic studies or to take a steady job. One day I hope – and believe – he will discover what it is he wants to do with his life. Meanwhile his parents are understandably worried. Their friends' sons and daughters are at university or launched on a career. Waiting for the late developer is not easy.)

19

ADOLESCENT BLUES

Dear Mr and Mrs Shelley

I doubt whether Jason needs to see a psychiatrist. The reason for his 'almost manic-depressive behaviour', as you call it, is that the adolescent blues are capricious in their influence. One day you are in the depths: the next you are seized with a euphoria that is as intense as it is unexpected. If we wanted to explain it, we would probably say that these are abrupt swings between despair and hope, the sort of changes of mood we continue to experience as adults but which are less dramatic because we have learnt to control the swing.

I kept a diary when I was sixteen, Jason's age, and it is full of these mood-swings. 'Felt really low today', is followed a few days later by, 'I got up at four o'clock this morning to walk across the fields in my pyjamas. The grass was soaking wet under my bare feet. When I was far enough away from the school, I started shouting anything that came into my head, including the whole of Madbeth's soliloquy, "If 'twere done when 'tis done, then 'twere well it were done quickly", that Chas had made me learn by heart. Then I sat on a gate and watched the dawn. I have never felt so wonderfully alive. A farm worker cycled by on the track but said nothing.'

I hope some of the boys here do that even if it is only in St James's Park! But I am not so foolish as to imagine that all adolescents feel the same. If I have learnt nothing else as a headmaster, I have become aware of the diversity of the adolescent experience. In a few cases the adolescent does need more expert help than the school can give. If these cases have a common denominator it is that communication has broken down completely between the adolescent and his parents. I am not sure why this happens but I have a hunch that it may have something to do with the ending of physical contact.

Some fathers stop hugging or kissing their sons as soon as the boy reaches puberty, as though the boy could make a similarly abrupt adjustment from feeling to intellectual analysis. I have seen a mute, rebellious boy sit on my sofa while his father calmly analysed where their friendship had gone wrong and have thought to myself, 'Why waste time with this logic? All it needs is a good hug.'

Jason has a bad bout of adolescent blues but from the school's point of view there is nothing abnormal in his behaviour. He is driving his housemaster round the bend but Mr Edgar has been there before and knows the territory. There are always some adolescents who need to go on testing the strength of the adult world, not because they want to rebel against that world as is popularly supposed, but because they need to be reassured that adulthood is worth achieving. If the adult world turns out not to have the strength of its convictions, what is the point of growing up?

From my point of view the problem that Jason presents is familiar because it is normal. If I am too inflexible in my application of the law I shall end up by expelling him. If I am too permissive, he will see that I do not have the strength of my convictions. If I am inflexible one moment and permissive the next, I shall be accused of being inconsistent. Adolescents have a sharp eye for inconsistency but a deliberate inconsistency is an inescapable element in helping them through their adolescent blues; not inconsistency in the goal you are pursuing but in the day-to-day response to their provocation. The art is in knowing when to be firm and when to be flexible and it is just about the hardest thing to get right. You may not like all the implications of the fishing metaphor but there are times when you need to pull the adolescent in and there are times when you need to give him more line. I have not infrequently turned a blind eye to a boy's peccadillos because I have sensed that it is not the moment to escalate the conflict between us. I had to place a boy of Jason's age on a final warning last term in an attempt to contain his defiant behaviour. Around eleven o'clock a few nights later, I was walking home across the park when I saw the boy walking towards me. We passed one another in silence as though we were strangers. After that he had one or two more close shaves but he survived. On the other hand, there have been times when I have turned a blind eye at the wrong time and parents have rightly complained that their son would not have got into serious trouble if the school had not been so permissive at an earlier stage. I should not be surprised if parents, who may have no experience other than memories of their own adolescence, sometimes make the same mistake.

The difficulty of dealing with adolescents is real but I do not think we should make too much of a song and dance about it. Parents have been doing it successfully for thousands of years. We exaggerate the importance of adolescent blues, hence the increasing use of the psychiatrist by schools. I am not opposed to the use of psychiatry when it is really needed; what I am opposed to is the use of psychiatric help in routine adolescent problems. Some schools are far too eager to refer the wayward adolescent to the psychiatrist, as though subversive behaviour was a crime against the State that could only be explained in terms of psychological abnormality. We had a housemaster who was for ever calling in the psychiatrist because he wanted to reassure himself (and me) that the adolescent aggression was not directed against him personally.

You ask what your attitude to Jason's behaviour at school should be. While no two cases are the same, the good sense of my parents' approach has been confirmed by my experience as a headmaster. In the summer of 1947, when I was just sixteen, I hit the bottom of the adolescent depression. My bloody-minded moodiness and lunatic behaviour caused my parents and my headmaster sleepless nights, which was exactly what they were intended to do. My mother sent me a telegram at school: 'Do cheer up darling love.' A few days later my father was summoned to see the headmaster. When they had finished their discussion, my father strolled with me across the green towards the open-air swimming pool. I said something about being sorry he had to drive all the way from London and he replied: 'That's all right. But I wouldn't push the headmaster too far if I were you. He seems to be at the end of his tether.'

Looking back, it was a perfect double act, though I feel sure it had not been co-ordinated. My mother's unconditional love and my father's practical politics were just what was needed to see me through the crisis.

I hope that this is of some help to you.

Yours sincerely

JOHN RAE

20

A-LEVEL CHOICES

Dear Mr and Mrs McBride

I am happy to explain our A-level choice procedure and to give you some guidance about Shamus, though it is important that he should make the final choice himself.

You are right in saying that at sixteen he is too young to have to reject so many subjects. It will be no consolation to you to know that your view is shared by almost every headmaster and headmistress in the country.

Specialization at sixteen is deeply rooted in the English tradition of education. The origin is in our aristocratic approach: the English do not believe that the majority of children are worth educating beyond the basic level; so the whole system is geared to cut-off at sixteen, with only an elite allowed to proceed to specialization. The result is that only 22 per cent of our children stay at school after that age. We are alone among advanced industrial countries in this. In Germany the figure for those who stay on is 86 per cent, and for Japan it is 95 per cent. Compared with our competitors we have an undereducated and underqualified population; and our elite is educated on such a narrow front that its members often have no mathematical or modern language skills beyond O-level. We wonder why Nissan can take such pride in its industrial relations; the reason is that management and workers are not divided into elite and proletariat by their secondary education.

What we need in this country is a broad curriculum for the fourteen to eighteen age group that contains compulsory elements such as science, mathematics and a foreign language; and a law forbidding full-time employment under the age of eighteen.

No government has grasped the significance of this central weakness in our educational system. I think the reason is that a confusion exists about educational standards. We dare not abolish A-levels because we fear that it will lead to a fall in standards, but we are confusing high standards with specialization. Anyone can achieve a higher standard if he specializes in three subjects instead of six. The criterion for judging standards should be the goal that is desired and in the modern world that goal is a broad combination of subjects, not narrow specialization.

While this weakness remains, no amount of educational reform will make us a better-educated or more competitive nation. That is of no immediate interest to Shamus except to explain why, unlike his contemporaries in the industrialized world, he will now have to stop studying so many subjects.

Our procedure for making A-level choices is this. In the spring of Shamus's O-level year, i.e. next term, he will be asked to make a provisional choice of three A-level subjects. The starting point must be what A-level subjects he really wants to study. When it comes to university entrance it is his A-level grades that will count and he is more likely to obtain good grades in subjects he enjoys.

If he knows what career he wants to follow, his choice can be checked against the A-level requirements. But a career choice does not always dictate specific A-levels. In medicine and engineering it does; in law it does not. A potential lawyer can study what A-levels he wishes, though we would point out to him that the study of law at university involves the ability to distinguish between what is essential and what is peripheral in the text he is reading, as well as the ability to express himself logically on paper, skills which the study of A-level history will help to develop.

This advice and the checking of career or university entrance requirements is the responsibility of the housemaster in consultation with the careers master.

Most boys of sixteen have no idea what they want to do for a career. The most important influence on them is not the school careers master but what you might call the occupational lifestyle of their parents and their parents' friends. We tend to think that this is only true of doctors' children but the influence of the parental lifestyle is much wider than that. It may not dictate a particular career but it will encourage a boy or girl to stay within the same type of career, in the professions, for example, or in the City. That is not a golden rule nor does it excuse the school from giving expert careers advice, but I am struck by the frequency with which children end up in similar careers to their parents, even though the similarity may not at first be obvious. I remember a prominent businessman who could not understand why his son had become a celebrated pop star, but in fact they were both entrepreneurs with a gift for spotting the next trend. Rarer but more intriguing are the sons who choose the careers that their fathers wanted to follow but did not, thus fulfilling their father's unfulfilled ambitions.

If Shamus has no idea what he wants to do he is normal, not lacking in ambition or motivation. He will be using his A-level course as a means of obtaining paper qualifications and as a training of his mind. Harold Macmillan's classics tutor at Oxford told the new undergraduates, 'Nothing that you will learn on the course of studies will be the slightest use to you in after-life, save only this, that if you work hard and diligently you should be able to detect when a man is talking rot, and that, in my view, is the main if not the sole purpose of education.' It may not be the sole purpose but it is a remarkably useful attribute in any walk of life.

What Macmillan's tutor did not add was that a well-trained mind is just as marketable as a vocational qualification. Parents tell me that they do not want their son to study classics at A-level because it leads to nowhere but teaching. What rot! The truth is – though I have never been able to persuade the classics staff to publish it – that the boys and girls who have studied classics are now among the highest paid of all former pupils. They are snapped up by international management consultants and merchant banks. That is not the only measure of a subject's value but it gives the lie to the popular idea that subjects such as classics lead only to the academic cloister.

There are some boys who want to study subjects or a combination of subjects that we do not offer. Like most schools, we operate a blocking system at A-level with four blocks from which the individual can choose his three A-level subjects. Popular subjects appear in two blocks, less popular in one. The availability of a combination is dictated solely by supply and demand. If only a few boys want to study Russian, we cannot afford the manpower to offer the subject in two blocks. I do not think there is a better system but inevitably some combinations are ruled out.

As you have already noted, some subjects do not appear at all. You ask why we do not offer business studies. There are two reasons and they are the same reasons for the absence of such subjects as general studies and British constitution. The first reason is lack of demand. The second is that I do not believe that these are sensible subjects to offer in a school where the great majority of pupils are going on to higher education. Though these A-level subjects are in theory acceptable as university entrance qualifications, in practice they are regarded by the better universities as soft options. If Shamus is competing for a place at Cambridge, for example, an A-level pass in business studies will carry less weight than a pass in history or mathematics or a language. Incidentally, I have yet to meet a businessman who believed that business studies at

A-level was a good preparation for a business career. The commercial community takes the view that business studies is only useful *after* the individual has had practical business experience.

Now let us consider Shamus's provisional choice. I saw him last week to get some idea what was in his mind. He said he was pretty sure that he wanted to do English and geography but could not make up his mind about the third subject. That is a common problem, particularly on the Arts side. He is not a classicist, nor is he keen on modern languages. That leaves history, economics and history of art. My advice is that he should take history. Economics is a much harder A-level than boys realize and requires at least some aptitude in mathematics. Shamus would find it hard to obtain a good grade (and remember it is *three* good grades he is after, because that is what his competitors for a university place will have). History of art is not difficult but like business studies it is regarded as a soft option and some universities will not even accept it as an A-level qualification.

History, on the other hand, is not regarded as a soft option and it is one of the few A-level subjects in which it is possible to obtain a high grade by sheer hard work. You may argue that that is precisely what Shamus has not shown himself capable of. Don't despair! The history teachers here are among the best motivators in the business.

These are tentative thoughts. It is too early for a firm decision so do not press Shamus to make one. The English system is bad enough without our making heavy weather of it. We will see how his mock O-levels go in March. A good O-level grade in history has little bearing on a boy's chances of doing well in history at A-level (in which it differs from subjects such as mathematics and modern languages) but it is a subject where nothing succeeds like success. If Shamus can do well in his mock O-level, that will give him the confidence to tackle the A-level course.

What I suggest is that when the mock O-level results are available, you and he should discuss the possibilities with the housemaster. The school needs to have all the provisional choices by the beginning of the summer term so that it can plan the timetable and manpower requirements for the new school year: but it is still possible for the choices to be changed at any time before the new year starts.

Yours sincerely

JOHN RAE

21

SEX

Dear Mr and Mrs Stoppard

You are not at all unusual. I found it so difficult even to contemplate talking to my children about sex that I never said a word. Heaven knows what harm I did or avoided by my silence. At least Timothy has raised the subject with you. You ask what aspects of sex education the school covers and what you should say to Timothy if he raises one of the topics you have listed. You may be surprised to know that you are the first parents in fifteen years to ask about sex education. That may mean that parents do not expect the school to do anything and take full responsibility themselves, but I doubt it. In my experience many parents do not know whether their children receive any sex education at school and take no steps to find out. I was certainly in that category. If I kept quiet, with any luck the subject would never be mentioned. But with the boys and girls here I have no such inhibition: I am not emotionally involved.

On the benefits of lessons labelled sex education I am an agnostic. I know what I want the benefits to be but I have no idea whether they occur. The principal benefit should be that the pupils achieve a degree of understanding and confidence which in turn will help them to make mature sexual relationships as adults. But there is no way of knowing whether there is a connection between sex education and adult relationships. It is possible that sex education may in a particular case make all the difference between a sexual relationship that works and one that fails because the partners do not understand each other's emotional and physical needs. Possible, but not certain.

I was once a believer. It is important that you should know why, because a headmaster's policies are profoundly influenced by his own experience. Men of my generation and upbringing had no sex education at home or at school. My parents made no attempt to enlighten me and the school did not even teach the simplest what-goes-where biology. When I was a new boy of thirteen, my housemaster's only advice was, 'If you feel temptation coming on, get changed and go for a run.' My first discussion of sexual intercourse was at the age of fifteen with a schoolfriend who claimed to have spent the night with a legless prostitute in Paris. My sexual awakening was entirely in the world of fantasy and masturbation. I wrote romantic poems to imaginary girls and gazed longingly at Betty Grable's legs in the local Odeon. I never learnt to dance, which in those days mattered. Such contacts as I had with girls of my own age were shy and gauche.

Living so much of my emotional life in my imagination, it was years before I had the confidence to show my emotions to another person. I took refuge in the male round of sport and beer. I was happy enough but there was a price to pay. My first relationships with girls were disastrous because the girls were little more than extensions of my imaginary life; they were characters in the fantasy, not real people with emotional needs of their own.

It was this experience of delayed sexual maturity that made me such a convinced believer in the importance of sex education. Like the rich man in hell, I wanted to send a messenger back to the young to warn them that ignorance would land them in the limbo of unfulfilled relationships. When I became a headmaster, conviction became policy. I was the enlightened despot, convinced that the overthrow of superstition and ignorance would increase the sum of human happiness. Nothing must be left to chance. Without consulting either my colleagues or the parents, I imposed a compulsory course that covered all aspects of sex, from what-goes-where for the thirteen-year-olds to films on natural childbirth for sixth formers. Accurate information and frank discussion were the keys to salvation. The school took it all in its stride, as schools will when a new headmaster proclaims his first crusade. Masters and boys reckoned that my enthusiasm would soon wane and they were right.

It is easy to see now why my attempt to impose enlightenment failed. I still think the goal was right; if you could help children to make mature sexual relationships as adults, it was a reasonable assumption that their lives would be happier. But I made two mistakes. I overestimated the ability of teachers and outside speakers to communicate the understanding and confidence that I wanted the pupils to acquire. And I assumed, without any evidence, that accurate information and frank discussion would automatically prevent the delayed sexual maturity that I had experienced.

Failure made me sceptical. The only thing approaching sex education here now is the topic of reproduction in the first-year biology course. Even that is probably too late. Once boys reach puberty, the last thing they want to admit to is ignorance of the basic facts of sex. Beyond those biology classes, we do nothing in a planned or consistent way. I am just not confident enough that teachers, whose expertise is in another subject, can handle with sufficient balance, understanding and wit the sexual topics that will be thrown at them by the sophisticated young. Nor are outside speakers a safer bet. I have heard two only who got it right and I will tell you about them later in this letter. For the most part, outside speakers fail to find the wavelength of their audience, never an easy task but especially difficult when you are dealing with such a well-publicized but intensely private subject.

Maybe I am too sceptical. Maybe I lost heart too easily; it

is possible that my ill-planned experiments in sex education did help some boys. I am also aware that in some countries where there is a full-time member of staff responsible for personal relations, sex education is handled in a more efficient way than in this country. Even so, I am now convinced that, whether we like it or not, whether we do anything about it or not, it is as parents that we will influence the sexual future of our children. Timothy is thirteen. Don't follow my example and remain silent. He has given you the opportunity. You should take it.

There is no school 'line' on the topics you have asked me about. I will express a personal view. I hope you will find it helpful.

MASTURBATION

By the age of fifteen, young men are sexually active; within a few years they will reach the peak of their virility. Masturbation is not a self-indulgence; it is a natural and effective way of controlling probably the most powerful instinctive drive they will experience. I can see no moral or medical argument for making a boy feel guilty about masturbating. Yet it was not so long ago that it was regarded by parents and head-masters rather as now, with much better reason, they regard the use of drugs. Masturbation would result in degeneracy, mental apathy, physical decay and even death. It is difficult to recapture the moral and psychological climate of Victorian England in which this attitude prevailed but almost equally remote is the atmosphere of the 1950s when in some schools boys' trouser-pockets were sewn up to discourage them 'playing with themselves'.

The authorities' obsession with preventing masturbation was ineffective. It was impossible to stop boys masturbating and, if my memory is correct, the cold baths and compulsory exercise that were intended as an antidote to sexual desire had exactly the opposite effect. All the school authorities succeeded

in doing was making themselves look ridiculous (never a difficult task) and making some boys feel unnecessarily guilty. As
guilt about one's own sexuality is likely to be a bar to sexual
relationships, the disappearance of this obsession at least
reduces the number of men whose hang-ups inhibit maturity.

Is that all there is to say on the subject? If a boy asks me or
Timothy asks you, do we assure them that masturbation
presents no problem at all? I do not think that would be my
response. Masturbation is a solitary act, relying for its stimulus
on the imagination or on pornography. That habit of mind
carried too far into adulthood could make it more difficult to
adjust to sexual reality. If making love is only another form
of masturbation, the woman will only be an object, pornography made flesh. Discussing that possibility can also help
to define what a mature sexual relationship involves; and it
can suggest that in masturbation, as well as in other aspects
of our sexuality, self-control can have advantages.

PORNOGRAPHY

Pornography is an aid to masturbation, a source of sexual
stimulus for men who are undersexed, past sex or just like
their sex in forms not readily available. You would think that
the young would have little need of it and in a sense this is true.
They do not share some adults' compulsive and humourless
interest in pornography. Nor, as far as I can tell, does their
interest stray far from the normal. They may buy soft pornography from the station bookstall or, as one twelve-year-
old did, ask their parents for an annual subscription to *Playboy*
as a birthday present, but they are unlikely to enter the
pornographic bookshop which caters for more exotic tastes.

Does it matter if a fifteen-year-old boy buys a soft porn
magazine? I know exactly how I would have reacted if I had
found such a magazine under my son's pillow when he was
that age. I would have said: 'I shouldn't bother with this sort

of thing if I were you. It's a waste of money.' And then having had a surreptitious glance at it myself, I would have suggested that he throw it away. What strange confusions fathers discover in themselves when confronted with their son's sexuality. I would not have minded his buying the magazine, but finding it, I would have felt obliged to adopt a mildly disapproving tone.

I recognize another ambivalence in my attitude. It is silly to fuss if a fifteen-year-old's sexual inquisitiveness leads him to soft porn. But where would I draw the line? I would have been more worried if I had found under the pillow hard pornography portraying sexual perversion; much more worried if it had been a video nasty of sexually inspired violence. All pornography uses women as objects. Yet when I find a fifteen-year-old with a copy of *Playboy* hidden in his O-level religious knowledge notebook, I find it difficult to take the matter seriously. Despite the inconsistency, I believe that straight pornography is harmless and bent pornography is not. Yet is it so illogical? The soft pornography appeals to a normal instinct; the hard pornography appeals to a facet of human nature that is abnormal and possibly dangerous.

HOMOSEXUALITY

Homosexuality is a subject boys are keen to discuss, their teachers less so. No doubt the boys' enthusiasm owes something to their desire to embarrass their teachers, some of whom they suspect of being gay. But they are also interested in and worried about their own sexuality. A contemporary of mine at school was known as 'Homo Harrison' from the age of thirteen. Last year he appeared at a Forty Years On reunion and was greeted with cries of 'Good old Homo', by men in their late fifties. I don't think there was ever any evidence that he was gay but it seems that a group of adolescent boys needs a statutory homosexual. Like those Russian soldiers from punishment battalions who were dressed in black to draw the enemy's fire, the statutory homosexual draws upon himself the gay jokes and jibes.

In the closed community of a boarding school, the statutory homosexual is a common phenomenon but I have known him appear, too, in the form of thirteen-year-old day boys. He reflects the anxiety that some boys have that they are homosexual, an anxiety that is not diminished by the changes in society's attitude. The danger of the single-sex boarding school is not that it makes boys homosexual but that it makes them think they are. Cut off from normal contact with the opposite sex it is understandable that their awakening sexuality should focus on one another. As Robert Graves pointed out many years ago when describing his own school days at Charterhouse, 'For everyone born a homosexual there were at least ten pseudo-homosexuals made by the public school system.' And for all those who outgrow the misconception, there are a few who discover too late or perhaps never discover just how heterosexual they are.

The lifestyle of boarding schools has changed almost beyond recognition since Graves's day but the schools remain male institutions in which women play a low status or peripheral role, as art teachers, matrons and masters' wives. Despite the fact that many more masters are married than used to be the case, the common rooms of boarding schools still contain men who are frightened of women or, in a few cases, openly despise them. Something of that attitude, misogynist rather than homosexual, can influence the boys. It would be good to report that pupils are only influenced by the balanced, mature members of staff but you and I know that this is not the case. For good as well as ill, the eccentric and the distorted have their disciples.

Boarding school increases the likelihood of homosexual relationships between boys or between girls, but whether they are remote and romantic or physical and intense, I doubt they are harmful or have any bearing on the sexual orientation of the adult. The seduction of younger boys by older ones is rare where once it was commonplace. The seduction of boys by masters is also rare though there are masters who become romantically attached to individual boys in much the same way as Lewis Carroll was 'in love' with Alice.

If parents are considering single-sex boarding school rather than day for their son, it is not homosexuality that they should worry about but the development of negative attitudes towards women, either frightened or dismissive. To suggest that boarding school boys always find it more difficult than their contemporaries in day school to make mature sexual relationships would be a ridiculous generalization. What seems possible is that some of them may take longer to adjust to a world in which women, instead of being peripheral or fantasy figures, make demands upon them, not only physical and emotional demands but demands for equal status and opportunity.

Should the school teach that a homosexual relationship has equal validity with a heterosexual one? I do not think it should. A school should teach tolerance and understanding but 'equal validity' implies that a homosexual relationship is as normal as a heterosexual one and by no twist of logic or semantics can homosexuality be described as normal. It is natural for those involved because it arises from their nature but it is not normal either in terms of statistics or in terms of the biological imperative to propagate the species. It cannot be said to have the same validity, the same worth as a heterosexual relationship. To teach children that, is to fall into the trap of trying to correct prejudice with a lie.

I think the way to correct prejudice is to emphasize that it is an over-simplification to classify all human beings as either heterosexual or homosexual. There seems to be such a diversity of sexual orientations not only in the population but even within the lifetime of a single person, that to talk of exclusive classifications is misleading. The coexistence of heterosexuality and homosexuality in one personality does not seem to be all that rare either. There is homosexuality in all of us and understanding that ought to make us less prejudiced, even though our predominant interest is heterosexual. I have little doubt that the almost hysterical prejudice with which housemasters and headmasters used to respond to the first hint of homosexuality among their pupils was caused by their inability to come to terms with the homosexual element in their own make-up.

SEXUAL MORALITY

Masturbation, pornography, homosexuality, all raise questions of sexual morality. We don't need to go in for heavy moralizing when we discuss them with the young but we cannot avoid the moral implications, not least because the young will not allow us to do so. To take an obvious case, video nasties are morally evil because they exploit the evil that is in us. Isn't that the true definition of evil? I am not a religious man but the idea of Satan seems to me morally and psychologically correct. The ultimate sin is to tempt others into sin. But condemning video nasties is the easy aspect of sexual morality.

You will not find such moral certainty on the question of pre-marital sex. How should parents react if they find that their seventeen-year-old son is sleeping with his girlfriend? If they look to the Church for help they will find an instructive difference. For the Roman Catholic Church, the starting point is moral theology: marriage is a sacrament and it alone sanctions sexual relations. The fact that Catholic teenagers may not accept the argument in no way undermines the fundamental principle that pre-marital sex is morally wrong.

The starting point for the Anglican Church is not moral theology but what is happening. Increasingly, young people have sexual relationships before marriage so Anglican morality must adapt itself to take account of this. It cannot condemn pre-marital sex because it has no basis in moral theology for doing so. Anglican morality moves with the times; the Roman Catholic Church tries to relate the problems of the time to a timeless morality.

When asked by their children about pre-marital sex, do parents argue from an absolute moral position or do they try to formulate a relative moral position that takes account of the change in society's attitudes? Or do they abandon morality altogether and offer only practical advice on contraception?

If as parents we were asked a multiple-choice question on how we would react to our sixteen-year-old son's sleeping with his girlfriend, what would be your answer and mine? Here is our choice: (1) do and say nothing, (2) give him advice on contraception, (3) tell him that what he is doing is morally wrong, (4) approve of his getting experience before he is married, (5) urge him not to sleep with the girl unless they are in love with one another, (6) tell him you do not mind as long as it is not in your house. And then we should ask ourselves the same question if it was our daughter sleeping with her boyfriend.

I like to think that my answer would be a combination of (2) and (5). My reason would be this. My secular morality is opposed both to being irresponsible about the consequences of your actions and to using other people's emotions for your own pleasure. That is a clear moral position to adopt and it applies to both sexes.

There is another way of looking at what in our credit card society we might call easy access to sex and it is the one that was adopted by the visiting speakers I mentioned earlier. Their arguments are a good point at which to end.

The first speaker was a Jesuit priest. He emphasized the danger to the individual and to society of a culture that encouraged the immediate gratification of desire. What gave his argument particular impact with the young was that he did not isolate sexual desire but saw it as only one of the aspects of our lives that was being distorted by the instant-access 'philosophy' of our society. The ability to postpone gratification, whether by self-restraint or by thrift, is an essential part of our maturity. A baby does not understand why he cannot have what he wants immediately and as parents we have no doubt that it will be bad for him if we give in to his demands. How illogical it is if when our children are approaching maturity we do not argue against the instant gratification of sexual desire.

The other successful speaker was a humanist, a medical consultant and the mother of a former pupil. From her secular standpoint, she put forward a similar argument. An important part of the joy of sexual relations lies in the anticipation, in winning and being won, in what in animal behaviour is still called courtship. Instant sex cuts out all of these and reduces sexual relations to a perfunctory act. The young man may be thrilled by his first conquest but his all too easy victory is unlikely to give him or his girlfriend any satisfaction. The immediate gratification of sexual desire can be as damaging to real sexual pleasure as the Victorian taboos and inhibitions we are so proud to have overthrown; it replaces guilt with dissatisfaction, suppressed emotions with shallow ones.

As you can imagine, the Jesuit and the humanist did not agree on whether pre-marital sex was morally wrong. But they did agree that inability to postpone gratification of desire was a mark of immaturity and that it could be particularly destructive in sexual desire. There is no way of telling how far the boys and girls were influenced by this argument but I know they appreciated these rare adults who were prepared to help them find a foothold on the shifting moral surface we have created.

Yours sincerely

JOHN RAE

22

PARENT POWER

Dear Mr and Mrs Peterson

You ask how many parents are on the governing body. The answer is that only one of the twenty members has a boy in the school. I accept that public opinion as well as government policy aims to give parents much stronger representation on school governing bodies and that the independent schools ought at least to consider how this should affect their choice of governors. You probably know that at this school, and some other independent schools, the composition of the governing body is laid down by Act of Parliament. We have no say in the appointment of nine out of the twenty governors because under the Act they are chosen to represent various institutions such as the Royal Society and the Universities of Oxford and Cambridge. We can decide the choice of the remainder. But let us put these technicalities aside and consider how your proposal would work in practice.

You would like to see half the governing body made up of current parents, two to represent each of the five years a pupil spends in the school. Each year-group of parents would know to whom their complaints and suggestions should be made. The result, you argue, would be to make the school much more responsive to the wishes of parents.

I have worked with two different governing bodies as headmaster and at one time or another I have been a member of the governing body of five other independent schools. In two of the latter – both preparatory schools – current parents made up at least half the governing body.

There is no doubt you are right in saying that a strong representation of parents on the governing body makes the school more responsive to their wishes. Whether that is invariably a good thing for the school is more open to question. The time scale of parents' interest in the school is short; that will make them impatient with inertia or delay, but it may also encourage them to support the wrong priorities, particularly in capital expenditure.

The immediate effect of the change you propose would be to put more pressure on the headmaster by shifting the emphasis of the governing body from finance and planning to the day-to-day running of the school. Parents are in a much better position to put the headmaster on the spot than governors whose knowledge of the school may depend almost entirely on what the headmaster chooses to tell them. Headmasters soon learn that the less governors know about what is actually going on in the school the better. That is not a flip comment. It is practical politics. As a new, young headmaster, I was naive enough to think that governors would welcome a frank confidential paper on the problems I was encountering with staff and pupils. They were superficially interested but I could sense by the enthusiasm with which they turned to the difficulties of obtaining planning permission for the new pavilion that they would rather I had not raised such matters with them. Their view of the role of the governing body was that it appointed the headmaster, supervised the school's finances and kept an eye on its achievements and reputation. Education was the headmaster's business. In twenty years as a headmaster, I can recall only a handful of discussions on education at governing body meetings.

You may be critical of such an approach but it is the one the older independent schools have long favoured. Governors are men of affairs, not experienced in education. They are

non-executive directors and, as such, are bound to leave the
everyday management of the school to the Chief Executive.
If they have made the right choice of headmaster this separation of powers works well. It places the responsibility clearly
on the headmaster and discourages governors from interfering
in areas where they have no expertise. The better the governors, the more they leave to the headmaster. And I have found
that the more powerful and talented individual governors
are, the less they are inclined to think they can do my job as
well as their own. There is nothing worse for a school than
governors with small minds and too little to occupy them.
Yet I fear that many independent schools suffer from such
people. Give me the busy head of a great corporation any day
rather than a local worthy or former pupil with time on his
hands.

The danger with this conception of the governing body's
role is that it is possible for the headmaster to disguise his
inertia or incompetence, if not for ever, certainly for too long.
It is here that parent governors would have such an important
impact. Almost all parental criticism of schools boils down to
one question: 'Why doesn't the headmaster do something
about it?' If 50 per cent of the governors were parents, the
headmaster would have to give an answer.

You challenge me 'to say honestly what effect parent
governors would have on the school's policy'. That is asking
a lot! You are asking me to tell you what I have got away with
because parents were not in a position to bring pressure to
bear.

The first thing that comes to mind (and I guess this would
be the same for all headmasters) is my failure to deal quickly
and decisively enough with teachers who are weak or idle. As
a parent, nothing made me more impatient with my children's schools than the reluctance of the headmaster or headmistress to sack a teacher who was manifestly inadequate. Why
is this woman who spends half the lesson weeping allowed to

teach my daughters O-level French? Why is this man who is unstable, if not insane, still taking my sons for Geography? Parents cannot understand why such teachers are not dismissed. Surely in any other walk of life they would not be tolerated for five minutes.

As a headmaster, I know the difficulties of hiring and firing teachers, but I also know how tempting it is to use those difficulties as a reason for avoiding confrontations that are awkward and painful and that may unite the teaching staff against me. With current parents on the governing body, I would at least have to produce convincing reasons for not sacking a bad teacher. I wouldn't like it but it would be good for me and for the school. And if teachers knew this was happening they would be much more inclined to jack up their own performance. I know that is my job but I don't do it well enough and I would welcome the pressure from parents on the governing body. I would also welcome the opportunity to explain why it is not always as easy as it looks to improve a teacher's performance or to find conclusive evidence for his dismissal.

Parent governors would cut through the headmaster's plausible evasions on other subjects. I am embarrassed – just a little – to think how adept I have become at answering awkward questions about the school with that disarming honesty that is designed to kill the subject stone dead. You must have noticed the technique at parents' meetings: a frank admission of our limitations, a touch of humour and a suggestion that there are nobler educational issues we should be considering. Do you remember that discussion about school food at last term's meeting? The pupils think it is pretty awful and parents doubt whether they are getting value for money. But I have no enthusiasm for the subject, so when it comes to parents' meetings, I try to prevent questions by belittling the subject in my introduction. 'Do please ask me questions on anything you like, even on school food.' That deters most parents but at the last meeting it was just my luck that the mother who lectures on dietetics should turn up. She was right of course; the nutritional value of the food is negligible. I gave her the old 'menu sent to the school doctor every week' routine but she was not impressed. She even quoted Milton on school food. '1644 Treatise of Education, which I am sure you have read, Headmaster. Milton says the diet should be "plain, healthful and moderate". The food here is certainly plain and moderate but by the time it reaches the boys, whatever was healthful about it has long since disappeared.'

She was the first person to make me take the question of school food seriously. I may have brushed her aside at the meeting but I did think about what she had said. But I *did* nothing. That is the point. There were always more urgent problems to solve and the bursar made it clear that he was not having a dietician interfering with his responsibility for the catering. Now if that parent had been a governor, neither the bursar nor I would have got away with it. We should have had to take action or justify not doing so.

I am sure you can think of other areas in which parent governors would have a similar impact. In discipline, parents would want more emphasis on prevention of 'crime'; they would demand a more thorough-going programme of health education, particularly on smoking, drinking and drugs. They would take me to task for failing to see that all the members of staff supported the 'party line' on disciplinary matters. And I can hear them saying that the devil makes work for idle hands so there needs to be a more efficient and diverse programme of out-of-school activities.

I hope you see what I mean when I say that parent governors would focus the attention of governing body meetings on to immediate educational concerns, and that this in turn would put more pressure on the headmaster to solve the every-day problems which, unlike the Five Year Plan, affect the lives of the pupils in the school at the moment.

On the face of it, these must be changes for the better. But there is a danger. I have sat on governing bodies where parents were strongly represented. The parents not only wanted to interfere by dictating to the headmaster how he should solve the problems they had identified; some of them, I am sure, enjoyed humiliating him. As parents, they had – as one of them put it – 'to lick his arse' to ensure their children's careers prospered; as governors, it was they who held the whip hand. The man they had not dared offend because their children were in his power was now their servant. They could taunt him at meetings. They could demand explanations. They could move a motion for his dismissal.

Headmasters and headmistresses are fair game. I recognize that. A degree of headmaster-baiting goes on in any governing body meeting. We all seem to have hang-ups from our school-days and find it difficult as adults to meet headmasters or headmistresses without feelings of uneasiness and thoughts of revenge. We are not sure for what exactly but there is nothing we would like more than to see them crawl. That much is a normal hazard of a headmaster's life. He learns to be wary because the deference with which he is greeted hides a strong desire to make him look a fool. But load the governing body with parents and you could change routine headmaster-baiting into a personal vendetta.

I have seen it happen. Dissatisfied parents intrigued with the former headmaster to undermine the current headmaster's position. The proper business of the governing body was set aside so that petty complaints about the headmaster could be aired. I cannot believe that the best interests of the pupils and the parents were well served. The non-parent governors managed to stop it but not without a bitter row and the resignation of several of the parents on the governing body.

That is the down side of your proposal. It is not bound to happen however, whereas the advantages of parent governors would be certain. The headmaster would no longer be able to drag his feet, particularly on the question of incompetent teachers. I think that would be the greatest gain. The shift of power from headmaster to parents would be resisted by independent schools who would argue that market forces are all that is needed to keep the headmaster up to the mark. There is truth in that but the irony is that the most famous independent schools, just because they are so successful, are particularly impervious to parental criticism: the parents at these schools are so relieved their son has gained admission, they regard making a complaint as little short of blasphemy.

That is all changing as parents become more conscious of value for money but it is not changing fast enough. So I am inclined to support your proposal. Whether what we want will ever be achieved in the independent sector I have my doubts, though the example of the maintained schools may force our hand. The composition of the governing bodies of independent schools is anyway open to criticism. I have been fortunate in my governors but too many schools fill vacancies on their governing bodies with superannuated major-generals and fey clergymen who may look good on the notepaper but have nothing else to contribute. It is time someone made the case for filling those vacancies with parents. Why don't you persuade your MP to ask the Minister during the debates on the Education Bill whether the requirement that parents should be well represented on governing bodies applies to independent schools? The answer will be no but you will have succeeded in bringing the issue into the open; and my guess is that parents with children at independent schools will not let it be swept out of sight again.

Yours sincerely

JOHN RAE

23

THE INSECURE AUTOCRATS

Dear Professor Romilly

Thank you for your letter. I have no intention of agreeing to your son's proposal that there should be a school parliament. A school is not and cannot be a democracy. The head is an autocrat whether he likes it or not, and if he does not like it he had better find another job. There are checks on his power but they are only as effective as he allows them to be. In an independent school like this, he has the power to hire and fire teachers as well as to admit and expel pupils. By his patronage he can advance or retard the careers of his staff. However much he may wish to present himself as a first among equals, he is not. His power, his responsibility for all decisions and his personal identification with the school suggest an autonomous guerrilla leader or – depending on his style – an absolute monarch of the old regime – 'L'école, c'est moi.'

I have pointed out to David and to the group of senior boys and girls who came to help argue his case that even if I felt inclined to do so, I could not share my power. A school parliament would be a sham. They want a forum for the expression of school opinion but that way lies frustration and cynicism, not the 'training in democracy' that you envisage. Whether you call them parliaments or school councils, powerless representative bodies are mockery. They appeared like mushrooms in the spring during the Sixties but they have died a natural death. To consult your senior pupils is prudent as well as useful. I reckon that over the years the head of school's advice has saved me from any number of tactical or political blunders. But to create a formal structure such as a school council is both dishonest and politically inept. However carefully you explain to the elected representatives that you retain the right to make the final decision, they cannot understand why a unanimous vote to abolish school uniform has no effect whatsoever; and if their discussions are confined – as they are in some schools – to whether the tuck shop should sell Coke or 7-Up, you are insulting intelligent young people.

The headmaster's power is indivisible. Power is a naked word which makes some headmasters uneasy: they prefer to clothe it in less unambiguous concepts such as leadership or management. But the power is real, especially in independent schools. Though it derives from the school's statutes, it is not the letter of the law but the headmaster's political will that gives force to his authority. The parallel with the monarch of the old regime is exact. A weak headmaster will soon find his will thwarted by powerful groups such as the housemasters. Given the legal position, there is nothing worse for a school than a weak headmaster; policy and discipline fail, the school drifts and the pupils suffer.

I would not say that fear of being thought weak haunts a headmaster but it is his most vulnerable point and his potential enemies know this. 'I'm afraid that will be regarded as a sign of weakness, Headmaster', the common room Iago whispers as the headmaster contemplates giving a likeable rogue just one last chance. It is not Iago's concern for discipline that prompts this advice so much as his desire to wrong-foot the headmaster.

The teaching staff are ambivalent about the headmaster's power. They want him to be a strong leader because that makes them feel secure but it satisfies their envy of his pre-eminence to see him momentarily unsure of himself. Teachers, whose job it is to impose their authority on children, can find it difficult to come to terms with being under authority themselves. The headmaster has to accept that one of his roles is to be the target of the resentment and frustration of teachers who think they have deserved better of the world.

To survive as a headmaster you need a combination of qualities: a thick skin, a quick wit, stamina, a steady nerve, political dexterity, a capacity for ruthlessness and a keen sense of the absurd. I sometimes wonder whether the governors who select a headmaster have any idea what qualities are required. In the independent sector the selection is usually an amateur business. Every school has a governor who loves playing the kingmaker; his follies and intrigues would be amusing if they did not saddle the school with his protégé for the next ten or twenty years. His fellow governors enjoy the sense of power that the selection process confers on them, while often allowing the final choice to be swayed by idiosyncratic or ill-informed votes. It is not just that governors fail to choose the best man for the job; often, the best man has not even applied, and the idea of head-hunting is anathema to these amateur gentlemen. The result is that in the last few years many well-known independent schools have found themselves with no credible candidate for the vacant headmastership.

Allied to this amateurism are a host of absurd notions, such as that to have represented Oxford or Cambridge at sport automatically endows a candidate with qualities of leadership. When I first became a headmaster, I was introduced to the only member of the headmasters' conference to have killed a man with his bare hands. He had served behind enemy lines during the war. I wonder whether the governors would have regarded *that* as at least the equivalent of having represented Oxford at rugby. Just the man, you might think, to get a firm grip on the school's disorderly elements.

Whatever his qualifications, every headmaster will feel insecure at times. I have – but I would have been a fool to show it. A headmaster's authority is partly bluff; no point in calling it yourself. At no time is the element of bluff closer to the surface than on the big public occasion. If the school chooses to be surly or unco-operative, there is nothing the headmaster can do about it. If he loses his temper or tries to identify ringleaders he will make a fool of himself. But a headmaster who is not prepared to stand up in front of the whole school and assert his power is not fit for the job. Things are easier now than they were when I started headmastering in the Sixties, but I am still keyed up for the occasion as I walk in at the back of the hall to take assembly. Some schools are docile. This one is not. Every assembly is potentially unruly. That is what makes it exciting. You learn not to give a hint of your own feelings. The paper on which the notice is written is placed on the table in front of you; held in your hand the slightest quiver would be visible at the back of the hall.

You can face anyone else's school without emotion. Nothing is at stake. But with your own pupils, every public occasion, however routine, is a test of your authority. My daughter, who was in the sixth form here, called these assemblies 'the headmaster's ego trip'. And so they are. You walk out of a well-taken assembly a little taller than you went in.

There are other tests of a headmaster's nerve, such as the plots and cabals of his staff. There are usually one or two middle-aged members of the common room who focus discontent; and much as you would like to kill them with your bare hands, you have to spend time and energy on the more subtle business of outmanoeuvring them.

These politics of survival are not as self-interested as they sound. I could do little for the pupils if I was the puppet of this group or that.

David's idea that the headmaster's power is used solely to restrict the pupils' freedom and to expel those who do not conform, ignores the fact that the most important use of that power is *on behalf* of the pupils, particularly in the hiring, firing and inspiring of teachers. Even when it is used to control the pupils, the power is being exercised for their benefit. As I have pointed out, a weak headmaster is the pupils' worst enemy, especially if he is not prepared to punish and when necessary to expel. One timely expulsion can save many other boys and girls from getting into serious trouble. Do you know Cardinal Richelieu's *Political Testament*? Probably not – the ruthless First Minister of seventeenth-century France is unlikely to be one of your heroes, Professor. But he is one of mine. He recognized that what led rebellious nobles to the scaffold was not so much their crimes as 'the indulgence of former kings'. An indulgent headmaster, while he may enjoy a brief popularity, will also be the cause of broken careers. When I first became a headmaster, I expelled four boys in the first half of the term. Looking back, I do not think I should have treated them so harshly; perhaps they were the victims of a former indulgent regime.

The power of hiring and firing teachers must also be in the hands of the headmaster alone. It is as well that you should understand the realities of creating a good team of teachers if you are going to support David in his campaign for 'more democratic government in the school'. The mechanics of hiring are simple. In subjects such as history or English, I have a choice of several excellent candidates. In some other subjects such as maths and physics, I am lucky to be able to put together a short list. I have sometimes had to appoint a dud knowing what I was doing but having no other choice. If the occasional dud is appointed at this school, with its generous salaries and academic prestige, think how many duds there must be in schools that have less to offer.

Firing bad teachers is more difficult than appointing good ones. There was a headmaster in the Sixties who told his staff at the beginning of his first term, 'I shall not trouble to learn all your names because a number of you will be leaving soon'; and he was as good as his word. (The survivors, fearing that they would be the next to go, carried out a coup with the co-operation of the governors and forced the headmaster to resign. His successor had an easy time. The hatchet man had come and gone.) But more often than not, incompetent teachers are protected by the head's reluctance to act. The single most damning criticism of headmasters and headmistresses is that they fail to dismiss teachers they know to be incompetent. No commercial enterprise could afford to tolerate such inertia on the part of its chief executive. Speaking of the boys, Dr Arnold said that the first, second and third duty of a headmaster was to get rid of unpromising material. He was wrong about the boys but he would have been right about the staff. The first, second and third duty of a headmaster is to get rid of unpromising teachers. I can think of no other walk of life, except perhaps the ordained ministry of the Church of England, in which it is possible for a lazy man to get away with so little for so long.

One reason for the head's reluctance to act is that the law requires proof and it is difficult to *prove* that a teacher is incompetent. But the most compelling reason is the head's own sense of insecurity; he fears the backlash from the rest of the staff more than he fears the complaints of parents. This is particularly true when the incompetent teacher is well established. Teaching is an odd profession; there is little in the way of career structure and the majority of teachers reach a plateau in middle age with no prospect of preferment. Some of these men and women continue to give their best, teaching with enthusiasm until the last lesson of the last day. They are true professionals. But every school has its quota of teachers who have lost interest. Disappointed, sometimes embittered, the only enthusiasm they have left is for stirring up trouble. These are the men and women headmasters so singularly fail to sack.

The insecure autocrat broods in his study, considering his options and hoping an act of God will solve the problem for him. If only Mr — would fall under a bus. Sometimes the incompetent teacher plays into your hands by striking a boy in a fit of temper or turning up drunk to his afternoon class. Sometimes he offers his resignation in the mistaken belief that you have summoned up the courage to sack him. When such unexpected good fortune occurs headmasters cannot keep it to themselves. A regular feature of headmasters' conferences is the private exchange of lucky breaks. The almost hysterical glee with which headmasters tell these stories indicates how much the failure to dismiss incompetent teachers preys upon their minds. It is no wonder. This is the most searching test of whether a headmaster will use his power for the benefit of the school rather than just to protect his own position.

How much have you heard about Mr Waterstone's departure? He was dismissed the year before David arrived but the reverberations are still felt. When I arrived as headmaster Waterstone was fifty-four and had just retired from his housemastership. He was already something of a legend, part calculating eccentric, part guardian of the school's tradition. He had the ear of the governing body and was a vice-president of the Old Boys' Association. Altogether a powerful figure in the small world of the school. He was also an incompetent, lazy teacher who had no intention of changing his ways. He ignored the instructions of the young head of department. He paid scant attention to the syllabus. He set written work only once in a while and took so long to mark it the point of the exercise had been forgotten by the time it was returned. Cut away the sentimental claptrap about his devoted and loyal service to the school and you are left with an idle and inefficient teacher.

I dismissed him at the end of my second year having given him two written warnings which he ignored. I expected trouble but I had no idea such a storm would blow. The boys whose examination hopes he had so consistently undermined were fiercely loyal to him. The school simmered on the point of rebellion. The common room petitioned the governing body for Waterstone's reinstatement. The governors were equivocal. The Old Boys openly called for my resignation. At the annual Old Boys' Dinner when the president proposed the toast of the school, a voice cried out, 'To the departure of John Rae!'

There were times when I considered how – without damaging my authority beyond repair – I could invite Waterstone to remain. But there was no way. I had to see it through even if Waterstone, like Professor Moriarty, was determined to pull me down with him. In the end he went and I remained. It was a bitter, bruising episode from which some of my relationships here will never recover. Though everyone knew that Waterstone was not worth his place on the staff or the salary he drew, they hated me for being the instrument of his departure. Do you think that a disciplinary committee would have dared to sack this man? Not for a moment. If Waterstone's future had been decided by democratic procedures, he would still be here. That is the justification for a headmaster's power.

A school is not like any other community. As headmaster, I have to provide leadership for six hundred adolescents as well as fifty teachers. The former are not ready to take part in government. The latter have the virtues and vices of a guerrilla band: talented individually but reluctant to recognize a formal chain of command. That is why my style of leadership is closer to the guerrilla leader than the monarch of the old regime. Despite the committees and the working parties I am not at ease with such formal structures. I would call my leadership 'personal'; David would call it 'egocentric'. I am more of a demagogue than a statesman. I see no harm in this. Every leader must use what gifts he has. Some headmasters have the attractive but somewhat ineffectual decency of bishops; others, the administrative skills of managers. If you do not like my analogy with a guerrilla leader, let me suggest two other models for my style of headmastering – the film director and the revolutionary leader. Then perhaps you will see why all this talk of democracy in schools cuts no ice with me.

The film director is an autocrat because, in the words of the great French director François Truffaut, 'he is the only one with the whole thing in his mind'. He, too, presides over a guerrilla band, a motley of experts, with even less sense of structure than a group of teachers. His vision of what the film is to become is the one unifying force. He cannot govern by consensus or committee. The headmaster is also the only one who can see how the pieces fit together. Even the best of his colleagues only have a partial vision.

The revolutionary leader plays a similar role: he *knows* where the revolution is going, his single-minded pursuit of that goal gives him absolute authority. There is an interesting passage in Edmund Wilson's book *To the Finland Station* in which Wilson describes Lenin as 'the great headmaster'. Lenin, Wilson says, 'was fond of his associates, he appreciated their qualities but it never occurred to him to doubt for a moment that he could tell them what they ought to do; and he could never relinquish the final responsibility for what was said or done by the group any more than the headmaster with even the ablest faculty, the most promising crop of boys, can submit to a vote of the school'.

At the risk of confirming your worst suspicions, let me end by telling you that I enjoy power. That doesn't make me the megalomaniac of David's imagination. Power interests me but I am not addicted to it. When the time comes to give it up, I shall do so without regret.

Yours sincerely

JOHN RAE

24

THE BEST CON-MEN
IN THE BUSINESS

My dear Susan

I am delighted that you are thinking of sending Tim here. It would be good to have my godson in the school. I am enclosing a copy of the prospectus. When you have read it make a date to come and see me.

Beware! Headmasters are among the best con-men in the business. If we were not running schools we would be selling London Bridge to American tourists. We are not trying to deceive you, just to pull the wool over your eyes. It is our job to present our schools in the best possible light and most of us are pretty good at it. Parents are predisposed to believe what a headmaster says; it is hard to associate the dark suits, the boyish faces and the streaks of silver hair with the morals of Madison Avenue. The popular misconception that head-masters are out of touch with the harsh realities of the market place gives us an edge.

The first thing to understand about schools is that they are in competition with one another. With independent schools that competition can be cut-throat. The motto of the independent sector should be La Rochefoucauld's famous aphorism: 'In the misfortune of our best friends, we find something that is not displeasing to us.' The scandals that rock your competitors are a matter for public sympathy and private satisfaction.

The competition starts with publicity material – the prospectus and the school's entry in the Year Books. Competitive advertising is banned by the gentlemanly code of the Headmasters' Conference but the publicity material can still be a minor masterpiece of the advertiser's art. While you are not allowed to say, 'Eton – probably the best school in the world,' or, 'Nine out of ten parents interviewed said they preferred Westminster,' you can and do make the same point implicitly. For such really grand schools the technique is understatement. Eton has one of the briefest entries in the Year Book and its prospectus is a modest document compared with the glossy brochures issued by less fashionable establishments. For the latter, the problem is whether to project a sub-Eton image of antiquity, royal patronage and famous men, or to cut their losses and emphasize modernity and freedom from the more fuddy-duddy traditionalism. Or, of course, a skilful blending of the two. Look out for phrases such as, 'The school combines all that is best in the Public School tradition with a thoroughly up-to-date approach.' Whether such statements bear any relation to the truth is neither here nor there (they almost certainly don't); it is the impression that is important.

For most boys' independent schools, the need to establish ancient roots and royal associations is paramount. (To their credit most girls' schools disdain this sort of snob advertising though the exceptions can be ingenious: '— Abbey was founded by William the Conqueror to commemorate his victory in the Battle of Hastings on 14 October 1066. It became the home of the girls of this famous Public School in 1822. . .') The competition to be the oldest independent school brings out the best in headmasters. I particularly like, 'Queen Emma, mother of Edward the Confessor, chose as the place of education of her son the monastic seminary that was to become in later times the — School. The School, therefore, in varying forms, has existed since the refoundation of the monarchy in 970.' Or how about, 'The school is coeval with English

Christianity'? The fact that almost every prospective parent has to look the word up in the dictionary is part of the advertising technique.

Just for the record the oldest independent school with a continuous history is Winchester, which was founded in 1382. Does antiquity matter? Not a jot, but headmasters shrewdly assess the English gullibility on the subject. Commercial firms exploit the 'long established' theme, though less imaginatively, so why shouldn't schools?

The independent schools' attempts to establish some link with the distant past are harmless, indeed they have a certain charm. Equally harmless and no less ingenious is the use of a euphemistic code similar to that used by estate agents. You know the sort of thing; if a house is falling down, it is described as 'in need of some modernization'. I have sometimes thought it might be useful to publish a code book for prospective parents, but you will spot most of the euphemisms once you get the hang of it. The bleakest, hilltop site becomes 'a healthy elevated situation', a cramped urban school assures you that it is 'well placed to take advantage of the cultural life of the city', weak academic results mean that 'the school emphasizes the importance of an all-round education', and if the school is miles from anywhere it will have 'unrivalled opportunities for adventure training'.

The sleight of hand with which headmasters adapt to changing times also deserves mention. Not long ago one school stated in its prospectus that it was a 'Christian foundation' and that all boys were 'required to attend worship in the chapel'. A few years on, short of boys and forced to recruit in the Middle and Far East, the headmaster changed the wording in the prospectus to 'the school has a long-established tradition of religious tolerance'. I cannot help admiring the cool manner in which realities are faced.

All this is innocent enough unless you take a very strict view of what constitutes an honest prospectus. Less innocent and less easy to disentangle are the tricks that schools use to make their academic results look better than they are. Here we enter the no man's land between skilful presentation and dishonesty. I do not think that most headmasters and headmistresses set out to be dishonest. But they do set out to mislead you by not telling the whole truth and hoping that you will jump to the wrong conclusion.

For example, a modest independent school might advertise its academic standard with the statement that '95 per cent of our pupils receive conditional university offers'. The unwary parent might be misled into concluding that 95 per cent of leavers go on to higher education. What does the statement mean? Do 95 per cent of *all* pupils receive conditional university offers or 95 per cent of those who apply? I know it must be the latter because even in the most high-powered academic schools it is unlikely that that percentage of pupils will be seeking university places. But if it is 95 per cent of those who apply, the statement tells you nothing about the school's academic standard. Those who apply may be only a minority of the pupils, say, less than half. Let us say that 100 pupils leave each year and that only 20 of those apply for university places. According to the statement, 19 of them – that is 95 per cent – will receive a conditional offer. It does not say how many of these meet the offer by obtaining the right A-level grades. It might be less than half. So that out of one hundred leavers, only nine (9 per cent) are going to university, which would give the school the lowest academic standard in the independent sector. No lie has been told, yet by skilful use of words a totally false impression has been given.

A similar technique is used for advertising A-level results. '93 per cent pass rate at A-level' is the sort of misleading statistic that schools publish and they are careful not to explain exactly what that means. Does it mean that 93 per cent of the pupils taking A-level obtained at least one A-level pass or does it mean that 93 per cent of the A-levels taken resulted in a pass grade? If it means the former, it could disguise very poor A-level results; if the latter, it *could* mean that the A-level results are good. You need more information to be sure. Some schools operate a ruthless cut-off at O-level which weeds out all those pupils who are unlikely to do well at A-level, with the result that only a handful of sure-fire candidates sit the exam. The same applies to the school's success in Oxford and Cambridge entrance. '100 per cent pass rate at Oxford and Cambridge' is no big deal when you discover that the school has allowed only the three brightest pupils to try.

So you need to know the school's policy and how many candidates there were before you can make sense of the statistics. You also need to know the percentage who achieved each grade. 93 per cent of A-level results at Grade E, the lowest A-level pass, is not an impressive statistic. When a school just publishes the A-level pass rate it could mean anything from academic excellence to incompetence.

Schools that are academically incompetent sometimes try another 'presentational device'. They list the candidates by name with the subjects they have passed at A-level alongside. There is no mention of the grades or the subjects that were failed.

In the face of all these tricks of the trade a prospective parent should insist on having the statistics of academic results set out in a form that reveals rather than disguises the truth. This means that you need to know the school's policy for admitting candidates to the exam, the number of candidates, the percentage of pass grades and the percentage in each grade. In a good school with a strong academic entry the A-level results would look something like this:

Candidates	A-levels taken	% of pass grades	%A	%B	%C	%D	%E	%Fail
100	300	97	43	29	13	8	4	3

What you should look at particularly closely is the combined A plus B score, in this case 72 per cent. At A-level the difference between A and B grade is small. If the percentage of A-level results in those grades is near 70 per cent you can be sure that you are dealing with a Rolls Royce academic establishment.

Don't be satisfied with one year's results; ask to see at least the last five. Ask too to see the breakdown subject by subject. Even the best schools may have a weakness and that subject may be your son's particular interest.

Headmasters and headmistresses will twist and turn to avoid being pinned down, especially on the results of individual subjects. Some will try to fob you off with a flurry of statistics that do not answer your question. Others will blandly apologize: 'I'm afraid the detailed statistics have to remain confidential but I can assure you that they are pretty impressive.' They know that parents who are anxious to get their child into the school will not press the point. Even the most determined parents will run into a stone wall behind the smile of infinite regret. It is like asking to see the balance sheet of the Vatican Bank. But as long as parents are not prepared to get tough on this issue, the best con-men and -women in the business will continue to get away with it.

The great statistics game is played in the maintained sector as well as the independent because parents are so impressed by – and therefore so easily misled by – examination results. In such an imprecise business as education parents cling to the few hard facts available. The difficulty of interpreting results is not just a question of spotting the tricks. You also have to see the exam results in the context of the school's entry. A school like this, with a highly selective entry, ought to achieve good results, but how do you compare this achievement with the modest results obtained by the local comprehensive which has to take all comers? It should not be beyond the Department of Education and Science and the Independent Sector to publish a parents' guide to examination results, including what sort of results parents should expect from different types of entry, but until they do you have to be persistent in demanding all the information you need.

One last preliminary step I would recommend. Ask the head to send you a list of ten current parents who are prepared to be questioned about the school. Never rely on dinner table gossip; one disenchanted or starry-eyed parent can give you a very distorted view. The head will almost certainly say that he has no such list and has no intention of creating one. But it is common practice in independent schools in the United States and should be so here. Without the list you can still try to identify the parents but make sure you have enough to give you a balanced view.

Forewarned and forearmed, you are now ready to visit the school. Remember we are experts in salesmanship. Don't judge the school by our disarming frankness. We will try to get the awkward issues out of the way before you have a chance to ask a question. Use your eyes and your ears. Your senses not your intellect will tell you whether it is a good school or not. If the headmaster shows you round, don't bother too much with the new buildings and the rows of computers. Watch closely how the boys react to what the headmaster says. Their expression is a rough-and-ready lie detector. Look carefully at the notice boards. Note the graffiti. Once, I was being shown round an Australian school and saw a four-letter word scratched on the brick wall outside the staff common room. Every school suffers from graffiti but a school where the staff do not care is in a bad way. Above all, enjoy yourself. Visiting schools should be fun. If the headmaster is being particularly pleased with his own performance, remember this true story.

A headmaster was showing parents round a boarding house during afternoon lessons. The party approached the house changing room, unaware that one of the senior boys was taking a shower. The boy heard their voices and, as he should have been in class, dried himself quickly and hid in a cupboard. In the empty changing room the mother nodded approvingly at the clean and modern facilities. 'And we have ample cupboard space as you will see,' said the complacent headmaster, opening the cupboard to reveal the naked boy within.

I much look forward to your visit. Let us hope we are in for a few surprises.

My love to you all.

JOHN

25

THE BEST JOB
IN THE WORLD

Dear John and Elizabeth

Thank you for your kind letter.

You ask how I feel. Now that the last term is over and it is time to leave, I cannot say that I feel anything in particular, just a little tired. It was time to go.

I almost cancelled the final assembly this morning because I thought I would break down. But I misjudged my own emotions. The school did not have sadness in mind. It was a cheerfully riotous occasion, with coloured balloons on the ceiling and paper streamers shooting across the aisle. After all these years of fearing that there would be an assembly I could not control (it is a headmaster's recurring nightmare), at last it came. I could hardly get a word in, so I stuffed my notes in my pocket, said, 'Goodbye' and made for the door.

In the Yard afterwards, I hung about. A few boys and girls came up to shake my hand, but most hurried by to catch trains, to meet parents, to escape. Few things empty as quickly as a school at the end of term.

As a headmaster, your thoughts and emotions are so geared to the daily drama of people and events, you easily fall into the trap of imagining that the drama is in large measure dependent on you. But a school has a life and momentum of its own, particularly an old school like this. Headmasters come and go.

And when they go they cannot expect the boys and girls to do more than cast a curious glance at the emperor without his clothes. If they think of the headmaster at all, it is to speculate on what the next one will be like.

So I am glad to be leaving young enough to do another job. I could not bear to retire to a country cottage and catch myself looking at the clock each morning to see whether it was time for school. Or, even worse, to be a former headmaster who cannot keep away, like an actor who is drawn back to the theatre of his greatest triumph. The simile is apt. As a profession, teaching is closest to acting, and as a headmaster I have often felt that I was playing a role. Did you know that Dr Busby, the great seventeenth-century headmaster, was destined for the stage?

Performance or not, I have enjoyed it to the full. It must surely be the best job in the world. There is such variety, such unpredictability and such provocative fascination in dealing with the young. I shall miss them, though I hope not too much or for too long. The company of the young, particularly the lively and articulate young, is stimulating but it is also flattering. To have all these bright young things pretending to hang on your every word all too easily encourages you to believe that what you have to say is interesting. I shall miss some of my colleagues but not all of them. And I shall miss the parents I have got to know well, such as yourselves. I wish it had been possible to be on such friendly terms with all the parents but that is an ideal that no headmaster can achieve. I think, perhaps, I should write a book to tell parents what I have really thought and felt about all those issues that have united and divided us.

Goodbye and good luck, particularly to Edward – I hope his school career will continue to flourish.

Yours sincerely

JOHN RAE

ACKNOWLEDGEMENTS

The author and publishers are grateful for permission to reproduce material from the following sources:

The Schoolmaster by A. C. Benson (John Murray Publishers Ltd, 1902)
The Life of a Poet by Charles Osborne (Methuen London, 1979)
Surviving and Other Essays by Bruno Bettelheim (Random House Inc., 1979)
To the Finland Station by Edmund Wilson (Martin Secker and Warburg Ltd., 1940)